Eco-Justice
Essays on Theory and Practice
in 2017

Eco-Justice Press

Copyright © 2018 Eco-Justice Press

All rights reserved. No part of this book may be reproduced or transmitted in any form or by any means electronic or mechanical including photocopying, recording, or by any information storage and retrieval system without permission in writing from the publisher.

Eco-Justice Press, LLC
P.O. Box 5409 Eugene, OR 97405
www.ecojusticepress.com

Eco-Justice: Essays on Theory and Practice in 2017

Authors:

Audrey M. Dentith, David Flinders, Sandra Lubarsky, John Lupinacci, Jennifer Thom, Agnes Caroline Krynski, Andrejs Kulnieks, Chris Reddy, Dan Roronhiakewen Longboat, Kelly Young

Cover design by David Diethelm, Eco-Justice Press
Photo by Sean-Estergaard

Library of Congress Control Number: 2018902556
ISBN 978-1-945432-14-9

TABLE OF CONTENTS

A NOTE FROM THE PUBLISHER

CELEBRATING THE CONTRIBUTIONS OF CHET A. BOWERS
    by Audrey M. Dentith, David Flinders, John Lupinacci, Jennifer Thom **1**

DEVELOPING ECO-LITERACY THROUGH AN INTEGRATED MODEL: A PRIMER FOR ECO-JUSTICE EDUCATION CURRICULA
    by Andrejs Kulnieks, Dan Roronhiakewen Longboat, Kelly Young **11**

IMPROVING LEARNING AND SOCIAL OUTCOMES FOR CHILDREN IN AN INFORMAL SETTLEMENT: A CASE STUDY IN SOUTH AFRICA
    by Chris Reddy **23**

BECOMING RESCUERS
    by Sandra Lubarsky **37**

LANGUAGE MATTERS: CULTIVATING RESPONSIBLE LANGUAGE PRACTICES THROUGH THE ECOJUSTICE FRAMEWORK
    by Agnes Caroline Krynski **45**

A Note From The Publisher

With this year of *Theory and Practice,* we acknowledge the loss of a friend, colleague and mentor to many. C. A. (Chet) Bowers passed away in 2017. His influence will be felt for many years to come, both personally and intellectually by many around the world. The first essay in this book eloquently expresses Chet's influence.

Chet's determination to express his hopes and fears for the future was not understood or misinterpreted by some, but his investment of time, energy and great intellect toward something he saw as critically important to the world, will in time be seen as a selfless act and a useful guide for the future.

Our thoughts are with Chet's family. We hope his new adventures will be as remarkable as the ones he shared with us.

C. A. Bowers 1935-2017

Celebrating the Contributions of Chet A. Bowers
Audrey M. Dentith, David Flinders, John Lupinacci & Jennifer Thom

In July of 2017, C. A. (Chet) Bowers (1935-2017), Advisory Board member and co-founder of Eco-Justice Press passed away. Bowers was internationally recognized as an American environmentalist and educational scholar. Over his longstanding and prolific 40-year career, he authored 27 books (five books for Eco-Justice Press) and 105 journal articles. He also lectured extensively around the world with works translated into Spanish, Chinese and Japanese.

Bowers, one of the most provocative thinkers of our time, advanced the fields of curriculum studies and environmental education in fundamental ways. His contributions to our understanding of culture and language as the roots of today's ecological crisis and his call for cultural and linguistic change have provided genuine alternatives for classroom and community engagement. In honor of Bowers, we offer this short essay to gratefully acknowledge and celebrate the enormous influence that his scholarship has had on the field of education.

Bowers challenged both scholars and teachers in environmental education, curriculum studies and teacher education. Specifically, he implored environmental scholars to think deeply about the assumptions on which the field is based. He argued that common approaches to environmental education draw on the same root metaphors (e.g., change as progress, the individual as autonomous, and nature as a machine) that have marginalized indigenous cultures and fueled the globalization of Western influence and cultural colonization.

In the field of curriculum studies and teacher education, Bowers advocated for schools to develop curricula that support sustainability, principles of eco-justice, and ecological intelligence. He asserted both the need to foster more relational concepts of intelligence and refute individual intelligence as the basis for school design, teaching methods and evaluation. He argued for the revitalization of the cultural commons which involved assessing which social and cultural practices from the past should be conserved and which should be revised (2011).

Bowers also addressed the urgency for ecologically sustainable school reform. Bowers maintained that not only do schools and universities fail to educate students to live less-consumer filled lives, they also do not recognize their complicity in promoting programs that are competitive, individualistic, and driven by consumer ideologies. In fact, he argued, schools and universities are at the very center of the crisis since they promote the technologies, research and practices that serve to deepen the environmental crisis we now face (Bowers, 2011).

Early Works

In 1974, Bowers published the book, Cultural Literacy for Freedom. This book, inspired by such works as Aldo Leopold's A Sand County Almanac (1949) and Rachel Carson's Silent Spring (1962), brought attention to how the ecological crisis, our cultural ways of knowing and importantly, education, were intimately connected. During this time, Gregory Bateson (1976), whose thinking also deeply influenced Bowers' work, argued that the major problems facing humanity were the result of the difference between how nature works and the way people think.

Now more than 40 years later, it is clear that Bowers and Bateson shared the same concern. This concern for understanding the ecology of mind, which Gregory Bateson addressed in the social sciences, cybernetics and semiotics, was the very focus sustained by Bowers' throughout his life as a scholar in education. In vital ways, it is Bower's insights and how he articulated these to scholars and teachers that have, in a most profound way, (in)formed the field.

On Relational Thinking

Four critical ideas raised by Bowers emerge from his questions about the integrity of relationality and interdependence. These concepts included: oikos, mind/intelligence, language, and map/territory. It was the understanding of these and other critical ideas that Bowers viewed as providing educators with alternative conceptual frameworks in which to make sense of how their assumed cultural ways of being and education writ large (re) produced cultural patterns. Bowers' conceptualization of ecology as inherently connected with the ancient Greek term oikos is foundational. As such, it not only enabled ecology to be understood as the study of natural systems and human impact on the environment, but also, the examination of cultures as ecologies. Theoretically, Bowers' integration of natural and cultural systems as living, nested and intersecting phenomena can be seen as germane to his deeper inquiry and identification of 'patterns which connect' (Bateson, 1972). He viewed educators as agents of culture(s) and through his scholarly work, Bowers revealed the implicit roles we play in the practices we carry forth and the impact of these on the world's natural and cultural ecologies.

Foremost, Bowers used the word ecology not only as the study of the behavior of natural systems, but also as a framework for explaining the nature of relationships. Relational thinking, in turn, relies on an understanding of the interdependent and interactive nature of all things. Ecology in this sense moves us away from forms of unilateral control toward an understanding of our interdependence. Bowers further challenged the idea of the existence of discrete entities and autonomous beings. Knowledge is shaped by both environmental and cultural influences. Individual autonomy, Bowers asserted, is an abstraction that, although widely accepted, is wholly false. Moreover, the failure to think in terms of relationships within an interdependent ecological system contributes to our failed understanding of what constitutes intelligence (Bowers, 2011).

Ecological intelligence, a concept derived from the work of Bateson (1972) stressed that intelligence is a mix of the recursive conceptual patterns that emanate from a person's ongoing participation in a large ecology of relations. Intelligence does not occur in the brain of the individual but is inherent within organic, evolving relations. Functioning at high levels of ecological intelligence requires a ubiquitous awareness of how ideas, values, and behaviors affect the wellbeing of all other participants in the web of life. Such thinking is reflective of patterns of thinking /awareness/ behavior that rely on all five senses, memory, recognition of cultural patterns and the differences communicated by others in natural and cultural ecologies (2010, 2011).

On Language

Bowers revolutionized educators' thinking about the environmental crisis by claiming that the crisis is a cultural one that stems from not only how we think but what we say. Our entrenched Cartesian mindset and our failure to understand the linguistic colonization of the present by the past ultimately prevent us from living ecologically-sustainable lives.

Two of Bowers' contributions include the need to understand the linguistic roots of our thinking and the ways that language perpetuates ecologically destructive patterns. He urged us to think of language metaphorically and to regard words as analogs that bring forth past ideas and practices which have led to ecological calamity. Thus, Bowers often reminded us, "Words have a history" (2013, pg.51). A person is born into the metaphorical language of their community and, as a result, adopts the ways of thinking that are constituted in that language. In effect, this is how, through language, one becomes dependent on ways of thinking that do not take into consideration the contemporary dilemmas that now plague us (Bowers, 2010, 2011).

Bowers went further and offered critiques of the industrial and digital ideologies of Western modernity and mass consumption—ideologies that continue to provide the conceptual templates and habituated cultural practices that today seriously threaten the sustainability of natural systems (Bowers, 2014, 2015).

The Cultural Commons

The conceptual basis for what Bowers (2006, 2013) called the cultural commons was another hallmark of his scholarship. The cultural commons have historically been associated with places (parks, libraries, airways, and public lands). Bowers extended this metaphor to encompass the shared knowledge found in creative works ranging from the arts, crafts, medicinal practices, indigenous languages, and folkways to agriculture, scientific research, and public education. He also spoke of enclosure, or the transformation of communities by market forces and privatization. The commons movement is a countervailing force against enclosure or the excesses of free-market capitalism. The significance of the cultural commons is that it underscores the pervasive but often ignored interdependence among people within the cultural ecologies.

Bowers, who was frequently misunderstood in his articulation of the cultural commons, did not intend for such practices to be romanticized. Instead, he thought that knowledge of the cultural commons would extend the basis for understanding our inherent interdependence in both formal and informal learning contexts. He also thought that our illusions of knowledge point to cultural patterns and blind spots to which we are unaware.

Bowers maintained that all teachers mediate between different cultural ways of knowing and among different generations that constitute the community of which they are members. Whether or not a teacher is cognizant or not of the choices they make in their classroom, they are, in fact, mediators who can offer information and cultural practices that contribute to an ecologically sustainable future. Choosing one set of cultural possibilities over another is a process of mediation, one that can lead to greater awareness of practices that support the sustainability of life on the planet (Bowers, 2005).

On Teacher Education

Bowers made the term ecojustice widely recognized in networks of higher education, community activism, and global politics. His contribution to ecojustice and teacher education—included his support of educators to learn to recognize and rethink cultural assumptions embedded in Western industrial culture in relation to their classroom discourse and notions about intelligence and relationality.

The significance of his scholarship stems from conceptual and qualitative research in K-12 classrooms, teacher education, and through global networks of political activism. He encouraged educators and activists to commit to critiquing the enclosures of intellectual engagement and critical foundations in teacher education and take into consideration the ways in which language and culture, via carrying forward patterns of the past, undergird the unjust and destructive social and economic ideologies and policies that constitute schooling and teacher education.

Bowers' conceptual work introducing the concept of ecojustice served as a foundational contribution to engaging students, and colleagues, in examining social and environmental injustice as inextricable. Bowers made explicit that education, and in particular teachers, played an important role in learning to address the unjust social suffering and environmental degradation as a cultural crisis endemic of Western industrial culture and thus one we could, and ought to, unlearn teacher education as situated in higher educational settings and political systems dominated by free market ideology. Bowers' work to revitalize the commons through ecojustice education in classrooms, schools, and communities continues to inspire major curricular and pedagogical changes in critical education (Bowers, 2015).

Ecojustice work in teacher education is central to teachers' understanding, and potentially challenging, the socio-economic conditions that create the illusions of isolation that undermine solidarity and the potential for teachers to be agents of change in support of socially just and sustainable communities. For many of the world's scholar activist-educators, Bowers' work opened doors that exposed the roots of Western industrial forms of enclosure and possibilities of revitalizing relationships through pedagogical projects that challenge the cultural assumptions opposing eco-justice foundations for teachers, offering opportunities to envision and embrace social justice and sustainability.

Bowers' work, as part of a cross-disciplinary movement, questioned the ideal of the rational individual as the nucleus of reflective thought. This conception of rationality has been widely attacked by feminist scholars as an illusion that glorifies the power of men, by behavioral economists as a poor predictor of action, and by cognitive and evolutionary scientists as neglecting our dependence on inherited patterns of thought and affect.

On Being a Mentor

On the topic of mentoring, we'd like to write in more personal terms, shifting here from our collective to individuals voices.

Audrey:

My experience working with Chet began just a few years ago when I contacted him to speak at an event at the University of Texas San Antonio where I was a faculty at that time. On the suggestions of a colleague, I had read some of his work and was intrigued. He agreed to serve as a Keynote at our event. I really got to know him, however, when he came back again for a more lengthy series of events in 2012. We collaborated to organize an intensive experience for graduate students in the Dept of Interdisciplinary Studies. We named our 5-day program (offered to students as well as the general public), the Academy for the Critical Inquiry of the Cultural Commons. Chet did a series of talks over the 5-day period for graduate students, professors, local community leaders and activists who responded, in turn, to his work. The idea was to foster a dialogue among activists, students and scholars who were committed to ecological and sustainable change. We offered films, demonstrations, and lectures. Local organic restaurants served food and our lively audiences exceeded 40 or more participants at some of the week's events. In addition to the events, we were able to secure funding to create a film on the week's events. The film described some of Chet's key ideas and his long-held desire to create a film on the cultural commons for students resulted from that week. Since then, I've replicated that program at my current university, Appalachian State University in Boone, NC in the summer of 2016. Although Chet was ill at the time, he managed to do a lecture for us via telecommunication. It's my hope to continue these kinds of forums in the future. Chet will always be with us in spirit as it's his work that will inform the foundation of these academies.

Chet was an amazing mentor to me. As someone new to his work, he spent a lot of time suggesting books, and offering support and encouragement along with opportunities for research and co-authorship. It was not uncommon for me to receive lengthy emails with advice and thoughts from this seasoned scholar. He was quick to promote my work and was always eager to speak to the students and teachers in my classes. He was also incredibly patient, explaining his ideas repeatedly to me and those audiences unfamiliar with them. I will always be grateful for his kind patience with me as I grappled with his compelling and complex ideas. His work has shaped my own in fundamental ways and his ideas are now at the forefront of my own thinking.

Chet taught me to be a more discerning critic of contemporary scholarship in education. He used work from a wide variety of fields and thought it was very important to consider the thoughts of others outside the field of education. As a result of his efforts and his very provocative ideas, he himself was often the target of criticism. He took it all in stride and was known to frequently lament that he was always "pushing against the wind".

Chet was admired by my colleagues and my family not only for his scholarship and reputation as a thinker, but also for his gentle and thoughtful manner. He will be sorely missed.

Dave:

My own collaboration with Chet began shortly after I joined the faculty as an Assistant Professor at the University of Oregon. Before I actually met Chet face-to-face, I had heard his department colleagues describe Chet as "the guy who writes books." Being new to the academy, I found this reputation a bit intimidating, and when we did first meet, Chet offered no pleasantries or small talk. He simply shook my hand, asked me to sit down, and inquired: "Who are you? And what are your intellectual commitments?" He might have well have asked, what are your ideas?—questions that were a bit scary for someone like myself with a very large but equally insecure professional ego. During my first year, Chet would drop by my office very occasionally to share his ideas and ask about my own. Sometime during the spring of that year, Chet knocked on my office door with an entirely unexpected question: "Would you like to co-author a book together?" I had never written a book and knew very little about how to do so, but such lack of confidence had not prevented me in the past from saying yes. My decision to do so in this case, now 27 years ago, would reshape and enrich my professional career.

Less than a week after Chet's invitation, he shared with me a draft of the introduction to what would become, Responsive Teaching: An Ecological Approach to Classroom Patterns of Language, Culture, and Thought, published in 1990 by Teachers College Press as a volume in their Advances in Contemporary Thought series. I hardly knew what to make of Chet's draft introduction, but it was clear that he was working with highly engaging, intellectually powerful, and socially far-reaching ideas. We established a routine in which each of us would separately draft consecutive chapters. Chet drafted Chapter One, I drafted Chapter Two, Chet Chapter Three, and so on. As each of us completed drafts, we would then swap drafts and edit each other's work. A pattern in our editing soon emerged. As I edited Chet's work, I would often take one of his (very) long sentences, and break it into two or three separate and shorter sentences. As Chet edited my work, he would take two or three of my short sentences and combine them in one long sentence. Somehow this routine worked out with good results, but I had to struggle to keep up with the fast pace of Chet's writing. At the time, it would take Chet about six to eight months to write a book. With my help, the book took a bit longer. But struggle I did, both to keep up with Chet's page production and to become familiar with the contours of his compelling arguments. Apprehensive and often befuddled, I absolutely loved co-authoring with Chet. I have never since experienced such rewarding intellectual engagement and productive colleagueship. And in the process, Chet also taught me how to work with publishers, what to expect from them, and what they expect from authors.

On a final note, it took me awhile to appreciate Chet's often playful sense of humor. In 1988, we co-taught a graduate seminar titled Ecology of the Classroom. At the close of each class session, Chet began ending class by saying "Goodnight David," to which I would reply in kind. We were playfully mimicking David Brinkley and Chet Huntley, co-anchors of the NBC Nightly News circa the 1960s. Brinkley and Huntley would signoff at the end of each nightly broadcast by wishing each other goodnight. Our younger students did not understand this cultural reference, so our own end-of-class signoff became more of a private (and, for me, endearing) joke. I close these individual comments with only half of that routine, writing with deep gratitude and sadness, Goodnight Chet.

John:

I first met Chet at an eco-justice retreat and conference in 2003. As a new master's student and high school Math teacher, I was searching for ways to bring my experience and passion for social justice and environmental activism into the classroom. Working then in Detroit as a teacher interested in the connections between social and environmental activism, I heard Chet at a keynote lecture he gave on "Revitalizing the Commons." My professor at the time, Dr. Rebecca Martusewicz, had assigned Chet's work to us in class and then encouraged a group of us from Eastern Michigan University to attend at the retreat in Miami, FL. Working now as an educational researcher and teacher educator in Washington, I will never forget those first days meeting Chet and how much learning from him over the years has contributed to several retreats, conference presentations, collaborative writing and research projects, and an unbelievable network of fierce scholar-activist educators who all similarly share a passion for eco-justice.

Whether it was talking about work or life, Chet was always an e-mail away and his communications were always filled with detailed feedback, suggestions, and next steps for organizing. While Chet's scholarship certainly stands out as seminal to a wide range of disciplines, his role as a persistent organizer, educator, and visionary thinker will have impacts that far outlive his bodily presence on the planet. Like the many others Chet mentored, I am eternally grateful for his generosity and patience over the fourteen years I knew him. Whether it was his advice to me as a new father or his sharp critiques of work I was reading and writing, I could always count on his guidance. Chet's bold scholarship and passion for the possibility and potential for cultural change was infectious and his prolific writing and extensive network of mentees and collaborators ensures that the work will continue well into the future. Rest in power, Chet Bowers.

Jennifer:

I am never more appreciative than when significance appears in the ordinariness of the everyday. Many of my experiences with Chet happened this way. It was the summer of '96 when I first encountered Chet—more specifically—his work, while doing some reading for my second graduate course. The book was not one he had written but The Web of Life by Fritjof Capra. Near the end of the third chapter, there was a sentence that caught my attention. Capra wrote, "C. A. Bowers has argued eloquently, language is metaphoric, conveying tacit understandings shared within a culture." (1996, p. 70) Jotting the sentence down in my notebook, I started reading Chet's work (there were already many books and articles), the writing of other authors whose ideas he critiqued as well as papers written by scholars who critiqued his ideas. My professor Karen Meyer, also the Director for the Centre for the Study of Curriculum and Instruction at the University of British Columbia, asked the class to nominate scholars for the upcoming summer series. Several of us put Chet's name forward and a few months later, we had the good fortune to learn from him in a course based on his then current book, The Culture of Denial. While the concepts in the title intrigued me, I was completely unaware of the profound impact they would have on my future learning, teaching and research.

When I arrived to class, it was standing room only. The next day, only a small group of us returned. At first, we wondered why so many students had chosen not to enrolll in the course. Yet as we continued to study with Chet, we realized that not only was his writing—which consisted of long titles and even longer sentences—dense with ideas that were conceptually challenging, the task of examining them deeply and practically demanded nothing less than interrogating our very selves. I also remember my meetings with Chet. He worried that although he could see direct connections to my interests in curriculum, he was uncertain how I might use the ideas from the course to inform my work in mathematics education. Two years later, as I prepared for my master's defence, I sent Chet an email to thank him and explain that I now had theoretical ways to make relational sense of issues within curriculum studies and importantly mathematics education which previously I could only point to and struggled to articulate as a teacher. It was this notion of ecological relationality that figured prominently in my thesis as well as my dissertation, has become strongly rooted in my sensibility as a researcher and evolved in so many generative ways as a result of my conversations, interactions and friendship with Chet over the past two decades.

Just months ago, I taught a graduate curriculum studies course for early childhood through to high school teachers. Chet and I discussed, as usual, which of his past and most recent writings would be suitable for the teachers. What occurred next were three unusual events. First, the themes of the papers that Chet and I selected for readings in past years always seemed to settle somewhere in the middle of the course. Yet this year, the readings were placed at the end. For three classes, the teachers and I explored the concepts in Chet's writing and worked hard to make sense of the meanings that the ideas occasioned for them. The second instance happened during the final two days when several of the teachers were visibly and emotionally moved as they expressed and heard others share how their thinking was changing them in unexpected and radical ways. While this was not uncommon to other years of teaching the course, somehow it felt different. I also could not help thinking that Chet would have jumped at the chance to be with us if knew of the conversations taking place.

Finally, before we gathered to reflect on the course, I opened my laptop to check the time. As I did this, an email appeared in the Inbox. One line of text was all that was visible but there was enough there for me to know that Chet had made his passage and he was "on his way to his next adventure." I looked at the text again and tears began to fall. Then just as swiftly, there was a sense of calm and a comforting feeling that perhaps Chet had been with us during those last days of class. For this and much more, I will always be grateful. Farewell Chet.

On Being a Teacher, Mentor, Colleague and Friend:

In closing, we want to note that Chet held a strong commitment to the communities in which he was a valued member. Throughout his career and retirement Bowers, as teacher, developed and taught courses that challenged and provoked his students to think deeply, relationally and always anew. As visiting professor, he traveled to universities, conferences and working groups for little or no pay to talk with students and community members about his work. Once there, Bowers eagerly interacted with the students and teachers in classes as well as his audiences.

Bowers was a beloved mentor to countless emerging scholars, professors and teachers. Quick to promote their work, he was generous with his time, always encouraging and supporting them through face to face meetings, phone conversations or carefully composed emails brimming with provocative ideas and thoughtful advice. As colleague, Bowers initiated and welcomed opportunities to collaborate with others whether it was to teach, research or write together. And as friend, he told stories about growing up and growing old, reflections on these experiences and how together, his academic work and life was constantly changing and evolving.

Since his passing, many stories about Bowers have been shared in the different communities and the world over. Remarkably, they express the same sentiments. Whether known as scholar, teacher, mentor, colleague or friend, he is described as having been a very kind, humble, fiercely tenacious, wildly intelligent and intensely contemplative man. For these qualities and for all of his important contributions he will be remembered fondly and with immense gratitude.

References

Bateson, G. (1972). *Steps to an ecology of mind.* Chicago, IL: The University of Chicago Press.

Bateson, G. (1976). Lindisfarne, Long Island, NY.

Bowers, C. A. (1974). Cultural literacy for freedom: An existential

Bowers, C. A. (2005). *The false promises of constructivist theories of learning: A global and ecological critiques.* New York: Peter Lang.

Bowers, C. A. (2006). *Revitalizing the commons: Cultural and educational sites of resistance and affirmation.* Lanham, MD: Lexington Books.

Bowers, C. A. (2010). Educational reforms that foster ecological intelligence. *Teacher Education Quarterly,* 37(4), 9–31.

Bowers, C. A. (2011). *Perspectives on the Ideas of Gregory Bateson, Ecological Intelligence, and Educational Reform.* Eugene, OR: Eco-Justice Press, LLC.

Bowers, C. A. (2012). Gregory Bateson's contribution to understanding the linguistic roots of the ecological crisis. *The Trumpeter,* 28(1), 8–42.

Bowers, C. A. (2013). *In the Grip of the Past.* Eugene, OR: Eco-Justice Press LLC.

Bowers, C. A (2014). *The False Promises of the Digital Revolution.* New York, Peter Lang.

Bowers, C. A. (2015). An ecological and cultural critique of the common core standards. New York: Peter Lang.

perspective on teaching, curriculum, and school policy. Eugene, OR: Elan.

Carson, R. (1962). *Silent spring.* Boston, MA: Houghton Mifflin.

Leopold, A. (1949). *A Sand County almanac.* New York, NY: Oxford University Press.

Developing Eco-literacy through an Integrated Model: A Primer for Eco-Justice Education Curricula

Andrejs Kulnieks, Adjunct Professor,
Trent University Peterborough, Ontario, Canada kulnieks@edu.yorku.ca

Dan Roronhiakewen Longboat,
Associate Professor and founding Director of the Indigenous Environmental Studies and Science Program, Trent University Peterborough, Ontario, Canada dlongboat@trentu.ca

Kelly Young, Professor,
Trent University Peterborough, Ontario Canada kellyyoung@trentu.ca

Abstract

In this chapter we draw upon an integrated model that fosters the development of eco-literacy as a primer for eco-justice education curricula. We draw upon multiple knowledge systems in order to promote sustainable environmental education practices and leadership development. Specifically, we focus on local knowledge advancement in an established Learning Garden Alternative Placement Program for pre-service teachers. We also consider how cross cultural, cross-curricular connections between scientific knowledge and Indigenous knowledge can be understood through engagements with learning gardens. We investigate an eco-justice framework to help inspire focal practices such as food sovereignty, gardening, food preservation, candle-making, and arts-informed eco-literacy in order to better understand the ways in which Indigenous and environmental education are interrelated.

Developing Eco-literacy through an Integrated Model: A Primer for Eco-Justice Education Curricula

Our collaborative research program has developed from our opportunities to learn directly from leading-edge eco-justice educators and their research (Bowers, 2003, 2011, 2012; Martusewicz, Edmundson & Lupinacci, 2011). Since 2004, we have attended various eco-justice retreats and conferences, and studied about the importance of bringing forth a cultural and linguistic analysis of the ecological crisis into teacher education programs. We have consistently embedded an eco-justice framework into our pre-service curricula that is mandated by the province of Ontario in Canada. As teacher educators, we believe that there is a need to extend curricular programing to include a critique of modernist language patterns, an exploration of local-global dependencies, and work to create a synergy between Indigenous and science based knowledge systems through an integrated, interactive model engaging multiple systems of knowledge into curricula. (Bowers, 2012; Authors, 2009/2013). The following diagram illustrates an integrated model for teacher education curricula:

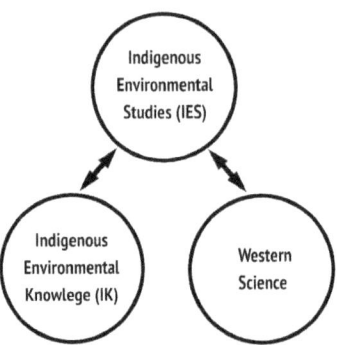

(Figure 1: *Integrated Model.* Authors, 2009/13)

By bringing together Indigenous Environmental Studies and Science (IESS) that promotes pedagogy based upon the importance of learning about local intergenerational knowledge through oral storytelling and experiential learning through a relationship between conventional Western Science with Indigenous Environmental Knowledge, pre-service teachers are immersed in two knowledge systems that help to promote an understanding of the interconnectedness of all Life.

This chapter arises from multiple knowledge sources as one of the authors is from Oshwe:ken, the Six Nations community on the Grand River Territory and is the founding Director of the Indigenous Environmental Studies and Sciences program at Trent University. The other authors are of European decent and are collaborative teacher educators and environmental and eco-justice education researchers who have spent years learning from both Anishinaabe and Haudenosaunee traditional teachings in order to inform their pre-service teacher education learning garden program at Trent University. For nearly a decade, as collaborative educators and researchers, we have been advancing a model for *integrated learning* (Authors, 2009/2013). By integrated learning we mean drawing upon multiple knowledge systems for curriculum development. We believe in the importance of including oral tradition, experiential learning, and traditional teachings as part of an established Learning Garden Alternative Placement pre-service teacher education program.

The Learning Garden Program

In 2012, we developed a Learning Garden Alternative Placement Program to help pre-service teachers integrate local knowledge into local schools and communities. Our program is situated in Peterborough Ontario at Trent University and Ecology Park/GreenUP in Peterborough, Ontario. Ecology Park/GreenUP is a not-for-profit community garden site that provides K-12 students with local environmentally focused curriculum programs. (GreenUP and Trent University are two partners in a regional multi-partnership that has recently received recognition as a "Regional Centre of Expertise RCE" for Sustainability Education by the United Nations University). Through a specific partnership between Ecology Park/GreenUP, Indigenous Environmental Studies and Science, and the School of Education at Trent University, pre-service teachers can choose to participate in a Learning Garden Alternative Placement Program as part of their degree requirements. It is through our program that we advance an integrated model with a focus on locally based knowledge through an incorporation of scientific knowledge and Indigenous knowledge that can inspire cross cultural, cross-curricular connections for K-12 educational practices. For example, through a series of workshops and field placements, Teacher Candidates (TCs) learn about food sustainability and environmental leadership through traditional Indigenous teachings from a local Indigenous knowledge holder and an expert gardener who understands the importance of tree care, native pollinators, caring for honeybees, plants, and vegetables, vermicomposting, etc. TCs participate in a number of different activities— curricula planning and development, and community outreach for the purpose of integrating local and multiple knowledges about the environment into their own classroom curricula.

> Ecology Park/GreenUP is a five acre showcase of sustainable landscape ideas and resources. With a host of display gardens and naturalized areas, a native plant nursery, children's programs, garden market, skill-building workshops and hands-on displays, the park has everything you need to be a good steward of the land in your care. (http://www.greenup.on.ca/ecology-park/)

With the support of community and university partners, we are able to offer a unique program involving local schools and a community learning garden to help prepare leaders in the field of education. Williams & Brown (2013) write:

> Through activities such as rainwater harvesting, planting of butterfly and other wildlife guilds, and providing insect and wildlife habitats, ... school gardens can teach children the value of connecting with and offering, human help to biotic neighbors. (p. 37)

It is during the program that learners can have deep conversations about food sustainability and their own relationship with natural places in order to better understand the ways in which all life is interconnected. We work to balance a theory-to-practice model that draws upon an eco-justice education framework (Bowers,

2003, 2011, 2012; Martusewicz, Edmundson & Lupinacci, 2011).

Bringing forth an Integrated Model through an Eco-Justice Framework

For the purpose of clarity, we begin with our collective understanding of *eco-justice education* in order to situate our research in the field. We turn to the Eco-Justice Dictionary for a definition of the term:

> The aspects of ecojustice that should be the focus of educational reforms at both the university and public level are connected with the need to reduce the impact of the industrial/consumer dependent culture on everyday life while at the same time ensuring that people are not impoverished and limited in terms of equal opportunity. (Bowers, 2004)

With the goal of eco-justice as a reduction of industrial/consumer dependency and social justice for all, we understand that teacher educators have two primary tasks of helping pre-service educators use an eco-justice framework in their classrooms. First, there needs to be a cultural analysis of the ecological crisis through a critique of modernist language patterns that perpetuate globalization and consumer dependency. This includes an integration or interaction of both Indigenous and Eurocentric knowledge systems. Second, educators need to identify diverse cultural methods that help learners recognize the ways in which eco-systems are being enclosed by forces of "development" and corporatization (e.g. food, water, land, air, etc.) in relation to the ways in which English language patterns carry forward modernist conceptions of human relationships with the natural world (Bowers, 2003).

In addition to the above definition, the Eco-Justice Dictionary outlines five factors when considering educational reform:

> …the five aspects of ecojustice that have special significance for educational reformers include the following (1) eliminating the causes of eco-racism, (2) ending the North's exploitation and cultural colonization of the South (Third World cultures), (3) revitalizing the commons in order to achieve a healthier balance between market and non-market aspects of community life, (4) ensure that the prospects of future generations are not diminished by the hubris and ideology that drives the globalization of the West's industrial culture, (5) reducing the threat to what Vandana Shiva refers to as "earth democracy" –that is, the right of natural systems to reproduce themselves rather than to have their existence contingent upon the demands of humans; ecojustice provides the larger moral and conceptual framework for understanding how to achieve the goals of social justice. (Bowers, 2004)

In our Learning Garden program, we pay attention to our local commons and natural systems that live in the places that we teach. Drawing on an eco-justice framework, we situate our research contextually by paying attention to *place* as central to our focus. With place at the center of our inquiries, we focus on the ways in which pre-service teachers are engaging an *integrated model* in their ongoing pre-service education. Our integrated model brings together Western scientific knowledge and Indigenous knowledge into a curricula that focuses on place as central to learning within the larger eco-justice framework. Within our pre-service program, teacher candidates draw on the knowledge of local Indigenous Elders and traditional knowledge holders, by spending time and engaging in traditional teachings, storytelling and cultural practice that includes a consideration of what it means to develop relationships with the places that they live. Cajete (2000) writes:

> An eco-education would draw from the knowledge, understanding, and creative thinking of past and present in order to prepare for a sustainable future. These sources are multidimensional, multicultural and multisituational. (p. 63)

Developing a relationship with local places involves a process of becoming *naturalized* to a particular place as learners engage in learning garden activities that involve food sustainability practices. Pre-service teachers work alongside an expert gardener-educator where they learn about the importance of biological diversity.

As we envisage the curriculum that supports the learning garden program, we consider one of the difficulties in understanding how to become naturalized within a particular place. To begin thinking about the local commons and how to develop deep connected relationships, it is important to consider the plants and animals that grow in places that one lives, but also, the stories and long history of the people who live there. Connecting with local Elders, knowledge holders and incorporating understandings about place from long lived, embedded Indigenous knowledge systems enables learners to imagine beyond a Eurocentric model that is solely dependent upon scientific knowledge. While pre-service teachers are learning about the importance of pollinators they can reflect upon stories told by Elders about our deep relationship with local landscapes. Unfortunately, the reality is that there are many things that are keeping learners from developing a deeper relationship with the places that they live. For Louv (2008), the issue is that young learners are increasingly not able to connect with natural spaces because they do not have an opportunity to spend time with these natural places. However, learning gardens provide opportunities for important connections to landscape. Williams & Brown (2013) write:

> It is often through direct experience and investigation of the flora and fauna, the soils, the seasons, the rhythms of natural cycles, the histories, and the communities within which humans live, that we develop and begin to feel a sense of place. (p. 61)

It is through our Learning Garden program that we endeavour to inspire a new generation of leaders in environmental education.

We believe that through an integrated model that brings forth local knowledge in pedagogical practices, pre-service teachers in rural settings are involved in the development of their own *eco-literacy*. Eco-literacy was introduced by David Orr (1992), who understands that "all education is environmental education" (p. 81), and therefore requires "the more demanding capacity to observe nature with insight, a merger of landscape and mindscape" (p. 86) It is through eco-literacy that we develop eco-intelligence, that is, the capacity to interpret the interconnectedness of all life with a deep understanding of human relationships with the natural world (Bowers, 2011).

One of the ways that we draw upon an eco-justice framework in our program is to engage in a workshop that examines the ways in which words encode earlier patterns of Western taken-for-granted thinking (Bowers, 2003). We consider the cultural assumptions embedded in languaging processes in terms of the abstract metaphorical nature of language steeped in enlightenment principles. We consider how dichotomies perpetuate systemic ideologies such as good/evil; light/dark; human/nature; man/woman; civilized/primitive; progress/tradition, economy/environment etc. (Martusewicz, Edmundson & Lupinacci, 2011). These hierarchized binaries privilege western anthropocentric enlightenment patterns of thought over all other forms of knowledge. We then engage in a pairing exercise whereby pre-service teachers match words such as forest/timber; landfill/garbage; stream/drain; insects/pests; soil/dirt; plants/weeds, etc. We identify mechanistic root metaphors and how we make associations and meaning through abstract language patterns (Bowers, 2003). By paying attention to abstract languaging patterns, it is our hope that TCs will begin to see the ways in which language has a history and is passed down intergenerationally.

In addition, we also have an opportunity to learn about Indigenous languaging patterns that are interrelated *with* local eco-systems as understood as *part of* natural local landscapes rather than abstractly outside nature.

Indigenous languages in North America for the most part, are largely verb based languages. Being such they provide descriptions of things rather than name it, naming creates a noun that objectifies and remains static and lifeless. Verb based languages are alive, they provides a description, a use, a relationship and often a story that is a reflection of that specific peoples cultural cosmology which recognizes and serves to affirm the life energy of the element you are identifying. A process of understanding and promoting Indigenous languages provides that deep connective relationship, sense of responsibility, and respect for Life that environmental education seeks to instill upon their students.

In addition to exercises about the historical roots of language processes and traditional Indigenous teachings, we include focal practices that foster the development of eco-literacy and local knowledge in our curriculum. We draw upon an eco-justice framework by placing an emphasis on place as part of the local commons (Bowers, 2003). By local commons we are referring to the ways in which Ecology Park/GreenUP is completely open to the community as all members of society are considered stewards of the garden. The learning garden does not have any fences or areas that are closed off to the public. Just as schools bring classes to learn in the garden from expert gardeners, all community members are welcome to explore and taste the vegetation that grows in the local garden. The stewardship of the 5-acre garden is open to all citizens with a hand-full of employees who oversee the garden and curriculum. For example, as part of the curriculum, TCs are immersed in school and community garden design, earth care through seasonal cycles, permaculture ethics that is to help foster positive attitudes toward food literacy and local ecological systems that are an integral part of biodiversity, cultural diversity, and building resilience. It is through an immersion in the learning garden that TCs develop a sense of wonder about the natural places where they inhabit.

Developing Deep Relationships with the Plant World

To begin to understand the limitations of only one way of seeing and being in the world, we limit ourselves to developing a deep connection to the places that we live. While science provides us with an overwhelming amount of data and information as content, it often times fails to provide us with a proper context. Indigenous teachings and long lived cultures of place provide us with both content and context. As the world is continually changing and people from all over the world are deciding to live in specific places, there is a desperate need to learn how to connect, respect and become responsible to care for the places we choose to call home. This need to develop relationship with each other and the world around us, to develop a sense of connection, purpose and a sense of responsibility is best illustrated through many of the traditional teaching of Indigenous peoples of that specific landscape. For us as the Haudenosaunee (People of the Longhouse – also known as the Six Nations) we look towards our teachings to provide us with multi-level, multi-dimensional and multi-situational understandings of Life. One teaching of the Three Sisters, whom we refer to as Corn, Beans, and Squash, is a reflection of how human beings need to work together to help, care, and share with one another. It also speaks to the responsibility to provide for future generations, to be connected to the entire world around us, from; the soil, to rain, to air, the sun, moon, and stars - we are connected to them all, and they to us. As well, the teaching speaks to the connection to our ancient past, as the seeds of the Three Sisters have carried us and we have carried them for thousands of generations and we have sustained each other. The Sisters are reflective of all women who are the sacred carriers and givers of life. The source of life that has created human life and how the sacred feminine is the foundation that sustains all Life. Most importantly how we are to give back to and care for the Earth (Our Mother), to learn to do our part to ensure that all Life will continue.

Focal Practices and the Importance of Developing Eco-Literacy

Traditionally, systems of schooling in Ontario, Canada, have been structured to view specific areas of the curriculum separately from one another. A decade ago, policy and curricular expectations were introduced to guide educators to infuse environmental and Indigenous Studies curricula across subject areas. For example, following the publication of the Royal Commission on Aboriginal Peoples (RCAP), The United Nations Declaration on the Rights Indigenous Peoples (UNDRIP) and the Truth and

Reconciliation Commission (TRC) Report's Call to Action, the Ontario Ministry of Education drafted a policy framework for Aboriginal education (2007) and resources for teaching about Aboriginal peoples (2009). Following this initiative, the Association of Canadian Deans of Education (ACDE) approved the *Accord on Indigenous Education* (2010) that embraces the importance of infusing curricula with Indigenous knowledge(s). The Ministry of Education simultaneously drafted a policy framework for environmental education *Acting Today, Shaping Tomorrow: A Policy Framework for Environmental Education in Ontario Schools* (2009). To support these policy initiatives, integration of Indigenous and environmental education across the curriculum is the focus of our evolving curricular programming.

As we consider how opportunities for teacher candidates to engage with a learning garden curriculum, we highlight the importance of an integrated approach to environmental pedagogies. When teachers ask students to work with the land that produces food they can eat, understandings about why they are learning can be enhanced and transformed. They become aware of linguistic meanings that engaging with the land can hold. Understandings about the land becomes a way of connecting ourselves with the earth. It also creates an opportunity to develop relationships with other students, but also with the plants and other life that surrounds us. We engage in *focal practices* by way of participating in arts-informed environmental practices that not only include gardening and the planting of traditional seeds and heritage varieties, but also preserving foods, candle-making, and ultimately eco-poetics, whereby learners reflect upon their own relationship with the natural world.

An example of a focal practice involves learning about bees. Hundreds of types of bees and insects are essential for the pollination of many of the foods that we (as humans) depend upon for our survival. Honeybees are one of the key pollinators that we ask students to think about as they consider the relationship of insects and the plant world. Honeybees are one species that has been in rapid decline due to an increasing use of pesticides and insecticides, ever-increasing pollution, and disease. There are many beekeepers across North America that are employed to move multiple colonies of bees to different locations during growing seasons to make sure that the pollination of certain plants takes place at key times of the year. One of the focal practices that can help learners connect with bees involves the focal practice of candle-making. The following photograph shows some of the equipment that can be used to introduce students to ecologically sustainable practices that can foster an interest about insect populations. By engaging learners in focal practices such as candle-making, they are learning about creative processes, energy production and not just the consumption of a finished product. Through outlining cross-curricular connections with the art of beekeeping, they are also learning about our dependence on the natural world.

(Figure 2: *Candle-making,* Kulnieks, 2017)

In addition to candle-making, developing eco-literacy is an important part of our learning garden program. Pre-service teachers are invited to write about their own environmental autobiographies and recount narratives about the natural places they inhabit. An example of a narration of natural experiences of childhood is captured in the poem *Blueberry Picking*.

Blueberry Picking
Kneeling on earth in blue-spotted corduroy pants
where grandmother and grandfather brought us toward
understandings about this special place

picking berries along forest paths
climbing trees in the wind
listening to spring-water flowing underground
like bubbles through sand—as snow melts

becoming aware of bee and hornet gatherings
as fasting brings us nearer to earth
walked by the four-leggeds and the other beings
who still inhabit landscapes…follow Original Instructions

What would the plants tell us if we would listen?
What would the animals say if we could hear them?

Gathering energy to be stored during winter months
plant and animal lives sacrificed so that we might live well
watching birds stop singing
staring up at Skyworld

> branches crack in the distance
> a language of interconnectedness
>
> searching sacred places
> finding mushrooms that return here in summer-time
> underground communities gathering since time immemorial
>
> memories of grandfather's stories
> reminding us where to look
> remembered rocks lead the way
> along the Precambrian shield
> becoming familiar with the trail of breadcrumbs left by generations
> as we look along the forest floor
>
> watching earth walked by spiders, bees, and ants
> in remembrance that we are not the only ones here
> as we share time.
>
> (Author, 2017)

This poem shares a story of walking through the forest and picking blueberries as a focal practice. They are personal and blend of witnessing a moment that also echoes years of engaging with particular landscapes, one which is predicated on the recognition of millennia of Indigenous interaction with place. They outline a story of growing and developing a relationship with the places they return to over a course of time, which is what happens when we ask students to re-conceptualize their understandings about the land that gives them life. As we theorize this work through collective our discussions, as well as our discussions with the Elders and knowledge holders that we work with, this process becomes a foundational part of our research. Our understandings influence what we hope TC's will think about, as their own discussions will lead them towards future lesson plans and investigations.

In the learning garden we engage in discussions about the differing relationships that we have with the land where we live and the plants and natural systems that give us life. We consider the different understandings that our TC students bring to their discussions as they engage with the land and consider how they will enable their future students to consider their relationships with the places that they live. We realize that brief reflections can be a beginning point of their relationships, but deepening understandings takes a good deal of time as it needs to provide both the critical content and most importantly, the context of place based learning. This face to face time with landscape is something that should be planned as part of curricular exploration. The opportunity to communicate both orally and literally is an important part of processes of learning.

Learning gardens like one used for the Trent University field placement for teacher candidates may be a return to witnessing how to grow food or it may even be the first encounter students have with rural gardening that is part of understanding intact ecosystems. This particular aspect that is not difficult in rural education, can also be replicated in cities. Competition and counting- based activities are not the key activities of developing deeper understanding of the lives of plants and animals. With an increasing number of students living far away from the soil an urban school systems we think that it is important for students to have a relationship with the things that they consume. Learning about the Earth through an active relationship with the places that they live and the stories that come from those places can help teacher candidates develop an understanding about the place-based research that they will hopefully continue throughout their lives. As learners begin to understand the pedagogy of place they can also deepen their understandings the importance of the Earth. As Cajete (1994) writes: ...the collection, preparation, and eating of foodstuffs from one's natural environment... is sacred and symbolic of that which gives us life..." (p. 105). He describes the process of connecting with our food as a foundation of understanding that sustains all Life.

Significance of Focal Practices in an Eco-Justice Framework

Learning gardens can connect the curriculum of Language-learning, Mathematics, History, Social Sciences, Science, and Indigenous Environmental Studies. Arts-informed focal practices can help learners to develop a deeper connection with place by recognizing and providing spaces for multiple learning approaches to explore the interconnected ways in with the places they live. Cross-curricular connections do not necessarily have to take place in the same year of study, although it is invaluable when they do. The important part is to make the cross-cultural connections on an ongoing basis, so that students develop a deeper understanding of the interconnectedness of all the different areas the curriculum asks them to consider.

As we ask our students to represent what they are thinking and writing about, we consider our own engagement with growing food, collecting and harvesting wild edibles, drying fruit, making candles, picking berries as intergenerational focal practices. We focus on the process of engaging with learning gardens as learners develop eco-literacy as a habit of mind and the importance of embedded learning. Ultimately, as educators and learners, it has been our experience that environmental education curricula in North America has been primarily based upon the scientific model of inquiry or a "Eurocentric" model (Battiste & Henderson, 2009) and that the result of solely depending on only that one perspective is not working well enough to hold the line on the environmental crisis. Education in an era of an ever-evolving environmental crisis requires a paradigm shift with a purpose of bringing forth a model that bridges and seeks to integrate both academic disciplines and cultural knowledge systems into a more integrative or interactive process engaging multiple knowledge systems. It is through this process that we can begin to address environmental complexity as resolving complex problems necessitates complex expertise. Our interest is to inform environmental education with an Indigenous approach through an integration of inter-generational knowledge via Indigenous teachings, philosophies, and languages that involves a process of focal practices in the learning garden.

References

ACDE. (2010). Accord on indigenous education. Retrieved October 8, 2012 from http://www.csse-scee.ca/docs/acde/acde_accord_indigenousresearch_en.pdf

Authors. (2009/13).

Author. (2017).

Battiste, M., & Henderson, J. (2009). Naturalizing indigenous knowledge in Eurocentric education. *Canadian Journal of Native Education, 32*(1), 5-18.

Bowers, C. A. (2012). *The way forward: Educational reforms that focus on the cultural commons and the linguistic roots of the ecological/cultural crises*. Eugene, OR: Eco-Justice Press.

Bowers, C. A. (2011). *Perspectives on the ideas of Gregory Bateson, ecological intelligence and educational reforms* Eco-Justice Press.

Bowers, C. A. (2004). The ecojustice dictionary. Retrieved January 25, 2015, from http://www.cabowers.net

Bowers, C. A. (2003). Toward an eco-justice pedagogy. Retrieved February 3, 2015, from http://www.cabowers.net

Cajete, G. (1994). *Look to the mountain: An ecology of indigenous education*. Skyland, NC: Kivaki Press.

Louv, R. (2008). *Last child in the woods: Saving our children from nature deficit disorder.* Chapel Hill: Algonquin Books.

Martusewicz, R., Edmundson, J., & Lupinacci, J. (2011). *Ecojustice education: Toward diverse, democractic, and sustainable communities*. New York, NY: Routledge.

Ontario Ministry of Education. (2009). *Acting today, shaping tomorrow: A policy framework for environmental education in Ontario schools*. Toronto: Queen's Printer for Ontario.

Ontario Ministry of Education. (2007). *Ontario First Nation, Métis, and Inuit Education Policy Framework*. Toronto, ON: Author.

Ontario Ministry of Education (2009). *Aboriginal perspectives: A guide to the teachers' toolkit*. Toronto, ON: Author.

Orr, D. (1992). *Ecological literacy: Education and the transition to a postmodern world*. Albany, NY: State University of New York Press.

Williams, D., & Brown, J. (2013). *Learning gardens and sustainability education: Bringing life to schools and schools to life*. New York: Routledge.

Improving Learning and Social Outcomes for Children in an Informal Settlement[1]: A Case Study in South Africa

Chris Reddy (PhD),
Environmental Education Programme, Faculty of
Education, Stellenbosch University

Abstract

South Africa according to Watson (2017) is one of the most culturally and racially diverse nations in the world in which education was governed by colonial and apartheid policies for a long time. Lotz and Olivier (1998) indicate that the change in government in 1994 has enabled fundamental change in the education policy environment in South Africa, which was primarily aimed at transformation at systemic, social and methodological levels. Johnston (1997) notes that educational policy changes are potentially far reaching in that the proposals for education transformation are situated within a broader strategy for national reconstruction and development. Watson (2017) indicates that education has this played an important role in galvanising the younger generation into an integrated society giving it a sense of identity.

While there is considerable evidence that education can increase income, reduce poverty and contribute to economic growth there is an urgent need to rethink the role of and approaches to education in different contexts in the country. Context based environmental education based on socio-ecological constructivism (Tidball and Krasny 2010) has significant potential to positively impact learners living in informal settlements, especially with regards to their motivation to learn and confidence to achieve both at school and in the broader community. Current formal approaches in schools exacerbate the disadvantages of learners in informal settlements, alienating them from performing optimally in the school environment. In this essay an argument is made for the necessity of adopting environmental education processes within communities to assist with improving performance among school learners and motivating for behaviour change in the communities.

---

1. unplanned settlements and areas where housing is not in compliance with current planning and building regulations (unauthorized housing).OECD 1997

Introduction

Few events in South Africa (SA) have been as dramatic and sudden as the demise of apartheid (the institutionalised separation of 'races' in all spheres of life) and the introduction of a majority, multi-party government by democratic process in 1994. The events immediately following the demise of apartheid prompted a series of changes in the political and economic systems of the country. While political reorientation and economic redress were of immediate concern, there was also an acknowledgment of the importance of educational change in the rebuilding of the country. During the apartheid period black communities were given schooling which prepared them for menial jobs. Ethnic identity dictated the mediums of instruction the type of courses offered and the institutions that people could enroll into (Watson 2017).

The scenario changed dramatically with the collapse of apartheid in the 1990s. While black communities still faced economic hardships they were no longer restricted by the government policies regarding education. Watson indicates that there were problems that emanated from the old era such as lack of proficiency in English that hampered development of a large percentage of the population. To this day most black people remain economically backward and cannot be part of the mainstream developments. In education this takes the form of restriction to enroll in premier schools as it is just unaffordable to the largely poverty stricken majority of the population. Watson (2017) further indicates the even after the demise of apartheid the policies that were in place and gave a disproportionate advantage to the white minority are still have a visible presence in terms of ethnic groups when statistics are drawn up and presented.

Stellenbosch (the town which forms the context of this research) remains a divided town where, two decades after the end of apartheid, people live in neighbourhoods that are still largely defined on the basis of race. The lack of contact between racial groups is reinforced by separate schools, workplaces and recreational amenities. Inferior schools and a highly segmented labour market restrict upward mobility for people. Poor public facilities in and around the informal settlement (name removed) mean that the prospects for social advancement and integration are slim without bolder efforts to transform conditions. Some churches have congregations in different neighbourhoods and make an effort to encourage social mixing. Overall, however, there is little exposure to the social lives of different racial groups and few opportunities to build mutual understanding and trust. Social tensions are reflected in Stellenbosch's volatile political situation, characterized by six regime changes in the municipality in the last 16 years, Seeliger and Turok (2013).

Maarman (2009:323) indicates that there is a plethora of issues to discuss in exploring informal settlement schooling in South Africa. He mentions that such schooling is characterised *inter alia* by low income, a lack of pre-school opportunities, socio-legal aspects which keeps people caught up in a cycle of poverty. Prinsloo (2004) further indicates that schooling in poverty stricken communities in South Africa is hampered by a lack of services, unsafe environments, lack of order in community structures, vandalism, negative peer group influences and an unstimulating environment that gives learners a negative academic self-concept that often lowers their level of motivation.

Globally, current thinking in education favours neo-liberal economic policies linked to a knowledge economy and South Africa has chosen an education path which fits this ideology. It was in the 1990s that globalization, a term coined by Theodore Levitt in 1985, became a household and regular term often called a buzz word. It is however difficult to pin down but essentially there is agreement that it has a multiplicity of meanings and impacts. The almost instantaneous communication possibilities have changed the world into what many call a global village. If people are connected they will be in touch and this many feel has made the mass media a powerful weapon to disseminate messages of choice – this in turn is what many believe has strengthened particular discourses to preferred status. The dominant discourses become hegemonic and develop into "Grand narratives" for global dissemination and currently include ideas related to neoliberalism and economic globalization.

Neoliberalism refers to a free market ideology that operates across political spectra (Aronowitz 2003). Essentially the term refers to the privileging of private interests and concerns over those of the public good. According to Sloan (2008), over the past two decades it has become a dominant mode of thought in western democracies and is market driven and not democratic. The ideas have radically re-shaped the way schools are structured and operate. There has been the imposition of business models and languages on public schools and this has pushed schools to adopt a factory model to ensure rational and expert decision making processes (Pinar 1994). Corporate values such as commercialisation, privatisation, de-regulation dominate the discourses of schooling for the past few decades and has led to an increasing privatization of education.

South Africa is no exception to these shifts and changes. Christie (2008) indicates clearly that the political changes and a change in government in South Africa happened in a time of globalization, something the former government did not have to contend with. This put paid to and made difficult the education ideas such as "opening the doors of learning to all". It was difficult in a globalized world which had standardized education processes and seemingly policies for the greater world. In a country where huge disparities exist socially and economically, such an education system has exacerbated the problems of inequality and thus the distribution of prosperity and abundance in South Africa. This is particularly relevant in the context of this research, an informal settlement, in an urban town, Stellenbosch, which will be discussed in detail later.

This essay draws on data from a community based study linked to two high poverty secondary schools dealing with all the factors mentioned above as well as the pressures of a national curriculum system. The case study data illustrate how through implementing environmental education processes, students' social context can be used to broaden the scope of the curriculum and enhance learning which can lead to progress beyond the narrow outcomes specified by the prescriptive school curriculum discussed in the next section.

SA Curriculum For Schools: Powerful Knowledge As A Curriculum Organiser

Curriculum knowledge and the structure of curriculum for schools has been widely discussed and debated in recent years. Given the context in South Africa it has been particularly relevant to this country. Christie (2008) indicates that changes in South Africa coincided with major changes in the world and the new government found itself in a globalised world where trends and changes were difficult to ignore or side step. One of the global trends in education is what Young (2007) refers to as the knowledge based curriculum. This is also coupled to an increase in centrally planned curricula which serve as National Curricula for the country. Bartlett and Burton (2007) argue that modern state curricula are likely to be derived from an amalgam of different ideologies rather than from one consistent and clearly defined paradigm. How curricula are conceived of and developed is linked to contextual factors which include social, economic and political factors that are supported by dominant discourses linked to power.

Osberg and Biesta (2003:84), in their text on complexity and representation in education, assert that modern Western schooling is 'almost invariably organised as an epistemological practice with knowledge firmly foregrounded as a guiding principle for education'. Young developed the notion of powerful knowledge which brings the epistemic and social considerations of social realism directly into relation with education (Hoadley 2015:741). What is powerful knowledge? Young describes powerful knowledge as the important knowledge that students need to know to help them negotiate the world and understand the world. It is also the knowledge that is valued for vocations and work places. Young further asserts that formal education serves to enable students to access (powerful) knowledge that is not available to them in their everyday lives and knowledge that enables them to move beyond their particular understandings and experience and gain an understanding of the world in which they live, (Young 2007,2013). Disciplinary knowledge contains abstract concepts that is separated from everyday knowledge and can potentially take human understanding beyond the particular and the local experience and conceptions, Beck (2013) in Hoadley (2015: 743).

Pinar (2004:xv) asserts that the key question remains: What knowledge is of most worth? He suggests that this is animated by ethics, history and politics and remains an ongoing question. He indicates that an important aspect of curriculum processes is to link the planned curriculum to the lived curriculum and to demonstrate to children that scholarship can speak to them and that scholarship can enable them to speak. His suggestion, in short, is that curriculum knowledge should be enabling and not alienating and that it needs to be mediated in terms of current living and life circumstances.

The national curriculum for schools has however evolved and changed as the policies developed met with contextual realities. This interaction often referred to as the policy practice or rhetoric reality gap forced curriculum planners and developers to rethink the ideas for the national curriculum. There have been three major curriculum iterations since the 1997 curriculum overhaul which has culminated in the current Curriculum and Assessment Policy Statement (CAPS) (Department of Basic Education 2011) which was used in this research. School curricula represent a statement of intent in particular subjects that need to be implemented in schools by teachers. Essentially these are statements of knowledge and ideas that are presented for discussion in the education arena / domain. EE has been included in all three iterations and has become part of the knowledge component of subjects like Natural / Life Science and Geography largely. This means it needs to be learnt in terms of the content / powerful knowledge of the subject / discipline in the CAPS document which is the current school curriculum.

This essay is based on research which was focused on a context based learning in a particular context in South Africa. The point of departure was that context based environmental education has significant potential to positively impact learners living in informal settlements, especially with regards to their motivation to learn and confidence to achieve both at school and in the broader community. Its action orientated focus involves high levels of participation creativity and community action all of which are effective at developing communication and general problem solving skills for learners. The context of the research is discussed in the next section.

Context – an Informal Settlement in an Urban Area.

The informal settlement in which this research was done emerged next to Kayamandi Township in 2008. This formal township represents the black section of the old apartheid town planners of Stellenbosch and is situated on a hillside at one end of the town of Stellenbosch. It is characterised by high density cheap housing with little in the way of amenities. The informal settlement evolved due to overcrowding in the backyard shacks of the formal township. As the backyard dwellers expanded their families in the formal township, so their need for additional space and facilities increased. Vacant land bordering the Papegaaiberg Nature Reserve[2] and the Plankenbrug Industrial area became a convenient area for many individuals and families to erect shacks. Due to political instability in local government at the time, insufficient action was taken timeously to curb the illegal invasion of land and the spread of the shacks on the hillside next to the Nature Reserve on land that was not suitable for

---

2. This conservation area is home to a natural vegetation type called Renosterveld which is critically endangered and only about 10% of it still exists in the region in conservation areas in the Western Cape Province.

low-income housing. By the time the municipality were ready to act and evict the illegal shack-dwellers, the number of shacks had grown substantially and translocation became politically unpopular (Swilling, Tavener-Smith, Keller, von der Heyde and Wessels 2007).

What has resulted ten years later, is a densely populated area with over 4,000 residents with limited access to public ablution facilities. People are forced to use the surrounding veld as a toilet. The area is a fire risk because of the density of the shacks, the use of unstable paraffin stoves as a source of fuel and the inaccessibility of the area to large vehicle. Solid and liquid waste removal is another problem. Inadequate facilities and arguably the lack of commitment on the part of residents to manage their own refuse effectively, results in open waste lying around for days before the municipality removes it. Moreover, waste water from washing and other ablution activities runs untreated down the dirt tracks between the shacks and into the nearby river, putting the informal settlement and the broader community at risk for waterborne disease, (Seeliger and Turok 2013).

There are several informal nursery schools operating in the area, not all of which are licensed. Children of school going-age in the informal settlement, attend one of the four schools in the township (there are two high schools and two junior schools). These state schools are supported by feeding schemes to ensure that children are fed. As many 10 people could live in one shack with parents and children often sharing a room. School fees are minimal in these state subsidised schools. Many of the parents of the children living in shacks have only part time or seasonal employment. Therefore, to survive, they rely on government sponsored child grants to feed their families.

While the local university and several non-governmental organisations (NGO's) have been operating in the formal township and the four schools for some time, few have ventured into the informal area. The children of the informal settlement are arguably among the most vulnerable group in the Kayamandi township of Stellenbosch because of their young age, exposure to a polluted environment, inadequate access to ablution and appropriate recreational facilities and opportunities. Parents in the informal settlement have expressed a concern about the influence that drugs and drinking in the informal settlement might have on their children (personal observation removed).

The Process For The Research / Intervention

It is against this background that a research project the Eco-Warrior Programme, co-funded by the City of Cape Town and the Cape Consortium for Higher Education was initiated. The Eco-Warrior Programme that Consortium for Higher Education Research project evaluated was borne out of concern for the cognitive, social and environmental disadvantages of the children living in informal settlements mentioned above. It emerged through the work of a non-governmental organisation in the area called Vuya Endaweni Community Conservation Partnership that was founded to protect vulnerable people and environments. The NGO that specifically focused on building positive relationships between children and their environment, had been running an environmental programme in the area informally for two years. They approached the Environmental Education Programme at Stellenbosch University (EEPUS) to help them evaluate their programme.

The focus of the programme was to teach learners about energy, water, waste and biodiversity within the context of their home environment – the informal settlement. From inception, the learners own context was identified as a reference point in their education. Firstly, only learners living in the informal settlement and attending, one of the two local high schools were permitted to take part in the programme. Secondly, the programme was conducted in the informal settlement at an education centre in the shack community not on the premises of the local high schools. Thirdly, there was an explicit focus in the material presented on the shack home and community environment in which the learners were residing. Fourthly, the material was focused on problem solving within their local context, empowering the learners to play an active role in their communities.

In each of the four modules presented there were four types of lessons, an information lesson on the topic, an at home application within the shack environment, a community application within the informal settlement and a final lesson focused on how the learners were going to present their findings to the broader community and bring about change. For example, the energy module included an initial lesson on the different types of energy (i.e. renewable and non- renewable), followed by a lesson on how energy could be saved within their shacks, to a third lesson where the learners conducted a survey in the local community on what types of energy the shack-dwellers were using and finally to a presentation by the learners to the local community on ways of conserving energy in the informal settlement. This action learning approach was thus firmly embedded in the reality of the learners teaching them problem solving skills to resolve some of the environmental and health risks in their daily lives.

The research project found that the action orientated focus of the programme boosted learner's confidence levels. They were required to actively contribute to knowledge acquisition by working in groups and going out into the community to talk to adults. Secondly, it developed a curiosity within the learners about their biophysical environment and their impacts on it. The learners actively searched for spiders, plants and even waste products to be turned into useful items such as small ornaments that could be used in the shacks. Thirdly, learners reported that they had a better understanding of the natural science curriculum at school following the completion of the Eco-Warrior Programme. Finally, the emphasis on having fun while learning, turned the lessons into social occasions and built friendships among the learners.

Discussion

Seeliger and Turok (2013) advocate for a better understanding of shack settlement dynamics in the context of the wider urban area and the longer time frame of the urban transition as an important consideration. They indicate that such settlements are nested in and shaped by larger more complex systems in which the existence of feedback effects or vicious cycles that can disrupt and destabilise the development trajectories of such systems. McInerny (2010) posit that the manner in which learners respond to school and other educational settings and the benefit they derive from these experiences is influenced by the socio-cultural environments in which they are socialised and schooled. Can (environmental) education assist positively in these processes? How can education processes be organised to be more meaningful and inclusive to children from informal settlements?

The Eco Warrior programme presented as part of this research had positive effects on the students and went some way to making learning more meaningful and enjoyable and less alienating. So dealing with students as a component of schools and a particular community is an important factor in processes that are aimed at improving the situation for children in and from informal settlements.

While the project was not modelled on the work of Tidball and Krasny (2010) there are definite theoretical positions that can assist in understanding the activities and learning processes observed in this project. These authors developed a framework linked to socio-ecological interactions and a form of what they term "civic ecology" as a framework for social constructivist learning in EE. In essence the ideas distilled were that EE programmes are nested within and linked to community based stewardship practices such as streamside restoration or community based gardening in their context. They draw on interactive and social learning literatures (Wals 2007) that describe learning as an outcome of interaction with the social and biophysical environment. They build the conceptual framework further by focusing on a particular form of urban environmental education they call civic ecology education (2010:4). This refers to programmes that engage participants in community based stewardship that can lead to engagement in the local environmental policy process, (Tidball and Krasy 2010).

The kind of activities and outcomes of the eco warrior programme had definite strands of this theoretical model and yielded positive community oriented results, with parents and learners working collectively on positive ideas for the context linked to the four themes presented in the programme. An unintended but hugely positive outcome was the revelation that this programme had assisted learners in better understanding the subject matter content of the school subjects they often struggled with. Tidball and Kresny (2010) indicate that civic ecology education considers urban areas as linked socio-ecological systems and focuses on restoration of urban socio-ecological systems. This provides opportunities for children to learn from the practical and diverse knowledge of different role players in the process and it is often possible to include other elements of environmental education including science learning, reflection on practice and communication skills. The underlying principle of civic education according to Tidball and Krasy (2010:5) is that rather than viewing humans as acting largely to destroy healthy systems humans can be seen to be nested within and able to take action improve communities and ecosystems. The underlying learning theory for this process of EE is that learning (civic ecology) is situated in interactive learning and social learning. Learning is situated in activity and occurs through interaction of a learner or group of learners with the environment including people, built and natural features of the environment and social and ecological processes. The project in this research had many such instances which yielded positive results for the community in the informal settlement.

Pillay (2004) worked with children from informal settlements who attended schools in areas outside of their places of residence but close to their homes. He interviewed children from informal settlements attending such schools to ascertain their experiences in the schools and to understand why they attended the particular schools. His research lifted out both positive and negative experiences of children. Common feelings expressed by students in Pillay (2003:6-8) included:

- Feelings of *fear and anxiety* because they were from outside of the area of the school.
- *Sadness* when insulted or made to feel different by teachers,
- *Loneliness* because they had few friends from the immediate area of the school and because children form the school did not freely socialise with them.
- *Shame and embarrassment* when they were unable to complete tasks and homework and were referred to in pejorative terms like *lazy, stupid* and so on.
- Misunderstanding – their demotivation was often seen as an unwillingness to learn and the real contextual factors were not known or considered
- *Envy* - Children from the informal settlement tended to envy the "luxuries" and facilities that the other children at the school had access to in their home lives which they often lacked in their own contexts.

A positive expression was that the children from the informal settlement felt a sense of pride at being in a school of "quality" and were of the opinion that they would receive a good education at this school that would improve their life chances. An important learning from this research we believe is that children need to be treated in a sensitive manner and that teachers need to take the circumstances of children into account when dealing with them formally and informally in the schooling context.

Mavuru and Namnarain (2017) explored the knowledge of teachers regarding their views of learner's in particular on the learners' socio-cultural backgrounds when teaching natural science. It resonates with the work we were trying to do in the informal settlement with EE and the school curriculum. They worked with three South African Township schools which are basically historically disadvantaged areas with poorly resourced schools in socio economically poor areas. Their research focus was on 'how do teachers accommodate learners' cultural norms, religious beliefs, socio-economic and political issues in their science lessons? Teachers in their project used their knowledge about learner's socio-cultural practices and beliefs to create opportunities to harmonise the conflict between learner's world views and science.

By doing this, the teachers it emerged provided authentic learning situations that promoted the development of critical and analytical thinking skills in learners.

They also started to include local issues and contexts to explain abstract science concepts to children. This is a sense was an approach which can be linked to the inclusion of *indigenous knowledge* in the formal school curriculum. Indigenous knowledge (IK) recognition and application is one of the principles of the current CAPS curriculum. The term IK is broadly described in various bodies of literature but we link to the work of Maila and Loubser (2003) who suggest that IK is knowledge embedded in the cultural milieu of all people. We also invoke the definition of Odora-Hoppers (2001:74) who indicates that IK is characterised by its embeddedness in the cultural web and history of people and forms the background of the social, economic and scientific identity of such a people. Mavuru and Ranmarain ((2017) indicate that by introducing indigenous knowledge into science teaching they found that science was demystified and becomes grounded in local knowledge which can improve student learning.

The Eco warrior project required learners to investigate local issues in discussion with comm8unity members and solo to investigate why the issues arose in the context. Much of the discussions with parents and other out of school persons provided background knowledge embedded in the local culture and norms of the informal settlement context which students were able to transfer to their schooling and activities linked to the school curriculum. We were able to link the everyday life experiences of learners to the learning required in the school curriculum and in our opinion this had a positive impact on the process of learning about and in the environment. Like, Mavuru and Ranmarain (2017) we endorse the views of Wertsch 1991) who indicates that knowledge is socially constructed and context dependent and that human mental processes are situated within their historical, cultural and institutional settings.

So knowledge of learners' socio-cultural background is an important knowledge domain for teachers to apply in school settings wherever they might be in practice. This would avoid what Jegede and Aikenhead (1999) refer to as the use of culturally insensitive teaching approaches, coupled with culturally unfriendly teaching materials and examples which can often adversely affect learner success in (science). This is particular relevant in South Africa where the knowledge based curriculum imposes a discipline on teaching through strong framing of the selection, sequence and pacing of school knowledge. Furthermore Beck (2013) suggests that powerful knowledge is not the whole answer and that there are enduring societal and educational dynamics at play that lock students out. According to Fataar (2014) abstract disciplinary knowledge and its power to change and provide opportunities does not always play out in the intended way and can lead to epistemic disaffection for many students in SA due to the large disparities and lack of opportunities for induction into powerful knowledge. This is particularly true for children from informal settlements with all its issues and problems discussed above.

Conclusion

Education has long been presented as a social process which can improve life chances of people. The narrowing of the education agenda and approaches to education that focuses on knowledge and predetermined outcomes has made these noble aims difficult to achieve. Essentially education has become a technical process governed by pre-determined outcomes linked to a strong knowledge representation in curriculum. The same knowledge based curriculum however serves as the policies for education across all contexts in countries and schools in more disadvantaged contexts have had a particularly difficult time responding to these curriculum mandates (Smyth and Shacklock1998). Current formal approaches to education in schools exacerbate the disadvantages of learners in informal settlements, alienating them from performing optimally in the school environment.

Although students in informal settlements are faced by a multiplicity of barriers that prevent them from choosing the educational experience they value we affirm that Environmental Education in a form of context based civic education can be a catalyst for improving learning and social outcomes for these children. Sadly, the lack of a follow up to the programme meant that the learners did not continue to receive the educational support and encouragement they needed. While the programme had the potential to change their lives, the once off nature of it was unlikely to bring about a lasting impact, except among exceptional learners who took these insights further of their own accord. What the programme did show, however, was the need to intervene in the lives of learners in informal settlement in a unique way. Instead of focusing on the deficiencies of their environment and their lack of adequate support but rather their extraordinary ability to flourish and survive in it, their self-confidence was boosted and their natural curiosity and interest in learning piqued.

Context-based environmental education linked to civic ecology practices has significant potential to positively impact learners living in informal settlements, especially with regards to their motivation to learn and confidence to achieve both at school and in the broader community. Its action orientated focus involves high levels of participation, creativity and community interaction, all of which are effective at developing communication and general problem-solving skills for learners as demonstrated in the social learning literature.

Reddy and Schreuder (2004:309) indicate that at this time in South African Education demands alternative frames of mind in the academe and in education practices. Given the transforming context they feel that scholarship in environmental education needs to express the critical nature of environmental education in ways that reflect the spirit and conceptual basis of EE that seeks to reduce current problems and prevent future problems and issues. It needs therefore to be broad and sensitive to contextual realities and to be focused on the public good. Context based EE / civic ecology education can provide the vehicle to make this a reality, particularly in resource poor areas like informal settlements.

Bibliography / References

Aronowitz, S. (2003) *How Class Works: Power and Social Movements*. New Haven, CT: Yale University Press.

Aikenhead and Jegede (1999). Cross-Cultural Science Education: A Cognitive Explanation of a Cultural Phenomenon. *Journal of research in science teaching* vol. 36, no. 3, pp. 269–287

Beck J (2013) Powerful knowledge, esoteric knowledge, curriculum knowledge. *Cambridge Journal of Education*, Vol 43: 177-193.

Berliner D (2013). Effects of Inequality and poverty vs teachers and schooling on America's youth. *Teachers College Record* Vol 115, 120308, December 2013

Christie P (2008). *Changing Schools in South Africa: Opening the doors of learning*. Cape Town: Pearson

Department of Basic Education (DBE), 2011. Curriculum and Assessment Policy Statement (CAPS) FET – Grade 10 – 12

Fataar A (2014) Access to schooling in a post-apartheid South Africa: Linking concepts to context. *International review of education* 43 (4), 331-348

Gulsen Kand Pedroni T (2011). Neoliberalism, cities and education in the global South / North. *Discourse: cultural studies in the politics of education*, Vol 32(5), pp 797-807.

Hoadley U (2015) Michael Young and the curriculum field in South Africa. *Journal of Curriculum Studies*, Vol 47(6), 733-749

Johnson, D. (1997) The challenges of educational reconstruction and transformation in South Africa. *Comparative Education*, 31(2), pp131-141.

Lotz, H. & Olivier, C. (1998) Clarifying orientations to learning programme development within the OBE curriculum framework and the Learning for Sustainability Curriculum 2005 Pilot Project in Gauteng and Mpumalanga. Unpublished paper presented at the Outcomes Based Education International Symposium, Vista University, 17-18 November, 1998.

Maarman R (2009). Manifestations of 'capabilities poverty' with learners attending informal settlement schools. *South African Journal of Education*, Vol 29,pp 317-331.

Maila and Loubser (2003). Emancipatory Indigenous Knowledge Systems: implications for environmental education in South Africa. *South African Journal of Education vol 23(4), pp 276-280*.

Mavuru L and Ramnarain U (2017). Teachers' knowledge and views on the use of learners' socio cultural background in teaching natural sciences in Grade 9 township classes. *African Journal of Research in Mathematics, Science and Technology Education, Vol 21(2), 176-186*.

McInerney D (2010). *The role of socio-cultural factors in shaping student engagememntn in Hong Kong: An ethnic minority perspective*. Hong Kong: The Hong Kong Institute of Education.

OECD (1997) Glossary of Environment Statistics, Studies in Methods, Series F, No. 67, United Nations, New York, 1997. https://stats.oecd.org/glossary/detail.asp?ID=1351

Osberg D and Biesta G 2003. Complexity, representation and epistemology of schooling. In B davids, T Fenwick, L. Laidlaw, E Simmit and D Sumara (eds). Proceedings of the 2003 *Complexity science and educational research conference*, Edmonton AB, University of Alberta.

Pillay J (2004). Experiences of learners from informal settlements. .

Pinar W (2004). What is curriculum theory? Routeledge: New York

Reddy C and Schreuder D (2004). Environmental education scholarship in a 'marketised' setting: a case study in a university environmental education programme. Environmental Education Research, Vol10 (3), pp 297-311

Seeliger L and Turok I (2013). Adverting a downward spiral: building resilience in informal urban settlements through adaptive governance. *Environment and Urbanisation. International Institute for Environment and Development. Vol 26 (1), pp 184-199*.

Sloan K (2008).The expanding educational services sector: neoliberalism and the corporatization of curriculum at the local level in the US. *Journal of Curriculum Studies, Vol. 40 (5), pp 555–578*

Smyth J and Shacklock G (1998). Re – making teaching – Ideology, policy and practice. London: Routeledge.

Swilling M, Tavener-Smith L, Keller A, von der Heyde V, Wessels B. *Rethinking Incremental Urbanism: co-production of incremental informal settlement upgrading strategies*

http://markswilling.co.za/wp-content/uploads/2015/10/Swilling-et-al-2013-Isandla-paper-first-draft.pdf

Tidball K and Krasny M (2010). Urban environmental education from a social –ecological perspective: Conceptual framework for civic ecology education. *Cities and the environment Vol 3(1): article 11.* http://escholarship.bcu/catevol3/iss1/11

Watson A (2017). *(https://plusgoogle.com/blog.findmypast.com/what cultural factors influenced the education system in South Africa – 2309382501.html*

Wertsch J (1991). *Voices of the mind: A socio cultural approach to mediated action.* Cambridge MA: Harvard University Press.

Young M (2013) Overcoming the crisis in curriculum theory: a knowledge-based approach. *Journal of Curriculum Studies*, Vol. 45 (2): 101–118,

Young M (2015) Curriculum theory and the question of knowledge: a response to the six papers, *Journal of Curriculum Studies*, 47:6, 820-837,

Becoming Rescuers
Sandra Lubarsky

Not long ago, a student told me that the Wendell Berry quote at the end of my e-mail signature convinced her to study sustainable development: "No matter how bad things get, a person of good will and some ability can always do something to make it a little better."[1] In fact, most students who choose to major in sustainability want to know how to be active and effective participants in transformative social change. They know that as privileged Americans, consuming far more of the world's resources than most people, they bear some responsibility for ecological decline. Simply hewing to the American standard of living makes us, willing or not, perpetrators of suffering. They also know that, to the extent that they are inheriting a mess not of their own making, they are victims. And they are overwhelmed by the extent of the mess and its complexity. But unlike many of their peers, they are neither content with things as they are nor willing to look the other way. They want to be rescuers. They don't use this language, mostly because they don't know it. But it is the identity they want and one that needs to be affirmed and reinforced as part of the teaching of sustainability.

We know that large-scale social upheaval is a precondition for genocide. And we know that most people consider themselves to be good people—even genocidalists. "People do not consciously arrange themselves along a moral continuum with the goal of defining themselves as evildoers or people who ignore the needs of others" writes Kristin Monroe, a leading researcher on rescuer behavior.[2] She cites Philip Gourevitch's similar realization in his chronicle of the horrors of the Rwanda-Burudi genocide: "People do not engage in genocide as if it were a crime…People don't go forward to kill saying 'This is the end of the world and I'm a pig and I will kill you.' They go forward and they say 'This is the beginning of a better world and I am a purifier and I will kill you. This is going to bring harmony.'"[3]

Making good and evil, kindness and harm the subject for careful analysis can help us to be less vulnerable to this kind of distortion and deception. Studying them together erodes the seemingly inexorable power of depravity and strengthens our psychological and ethical expectations. Most importantly, in giving attention to the literature of rescue, our students can come to know a set of agential possibilities that include the capacity to act responsibly and lovingly even under very, very grim circumstances.

Narcissism and Materialism

But we can't assume that our students will have the kind of moral frame or level of empathy that supports their desire to be moral agents and to act altruistically. Young American college students have been affected by the unbridled economism of contemporary American culture. Recent research reveals high levels of narcissism among millennials—students born between 1980-2000. A study of business students in the U.S. and the Netherlands found a correlation between increased materialism and increased narcissism, and then between increased materialism and lower environmental values.[4] A follow-up study demonstrated that even students majoring in sustainability showed increased levels of narcissism.[5] And because narcissism seems to accompany westernization, it is on is the rise worldwide. "As students, narcissists exploit others, are arrogant and haughty, and unable to empathize with others...Narcissists blame others for failures, take undeserved credit for success, are hypersensitive to negative feedback, and show an exaggerated sense of entitlement."[6] While the authors describe their studies as exploratory, they see a worrying generational trend toward higher levels of narcissism, greater materialism, lower ecological values, and lower levels of altruism.

Thinking in Particular about Particular Examples

To be intelligent in these times, suggests Wendell Berry, "you've got to have an array of examples you want more or less to understand. Some are not perfect, and others are awful, and to be intelligent you've got to know why some are better than the others . . . . .that means you've got to think in particular about particular examples."[7]

In an important follow-up to their narcissism study, researchers explored ways to mitigate this alarming shift among college students.[8] What they found attests to the importance of particulars. Students who had specific knowledge about U.S. policies related to human resources and labor protections (e.g., minimum wage, parental leave, sick leave, etc.) were more likely to support policies related to corporate social responsibility. Students who had little understanding of the fact that the U.S. lags well behind other industrialized countries in these areas of employment policy were less concerned with social corporate responsibility. Their conclusion: "Knowledge of social justice matters."

Further evidence for the importance of thinking "in particular about particular examples" comes from research on exposure to virtuous acts. A 2009 study by social psychologists Sara Algoe and Jonathan Haidt found that people who witness the behavior of "moral exemplars" are motivated to act in pro-social ways. In a series of studies, college students recorded their responses to various examples of "moral excellence," defined as acts of kindness and demonstrations of "humanity's higher or better nature." Not only did students report physical feelings of warmth and openness in response to their encounter with altruism; most significantly, they revealed a heightened motivation to "do good things for other people, become a better person oneself, and emulate the virtuous role model more generally." The authors concluded that, "Exposure to virtuous acts positively affects the way people view the world and, even more significantly, changes the way people act."[9] Though these studies were conducted under highly simplified conditions, they nonetheless provide quantitative data to complement the rich, qualitative studies (primarily interviews) of rescue behavior. And they give support for the proposition that it's a powerful thing to come into contact with particular examples of goodness, whether in the superficial confines of a social psychology study, through literature, or through direct, personal experience.

Social Relations and Rescue Behavior

When Holocaust researcher, Kristin Monroe asked rescuers why they had risked their lives to help strangers, they responded with bewilderment: "But what else could I do? They were human beings like you and me." What most surprised her was that bystanders also responded to her inquiries about their behavior with a sense of bewilderment. But theirs was for a completely different reason. "But what could I do? I was one person, alone against the Nazis," was their reply. How, she wondered, did rescuers and bystanders come to have such a profound difference in their sense of agency?

What Monroe found is that bystanders and perpetrators operated with widely different worldviews. Bystanders thought of themselves as individuals "alone against the Nazis," living in a world divided between "us" and "them," "insiders" and "outsiders." They harbored a sense of themselves as "embattled, under siege, wronged and/or needing to protect themselves."[10]

Rescuers held the opposite conception. They understood themselves to be members of a network of relations and part of a fellowship of human beings. Tony, a rescuer interviewed at length by Monroe, gave eloquent voice to this perspective: "[Y]ou're part of a whole; just like cells in your own body altogether make up your body, in our society and community, we all are like cells of a community that is very important."[11] This idea, that all of life is interconnected, is a central and recurring theme in rescuer interviews. It is augmented by the related belief in the preciousness of every human life and the need to treat every person with simple human decency. Often in the rescue literature, decency is expressed as hospitality, as offering shelter and comfort, not out of kindness but out of a sense of basic courtesy and a fidelity to the principle—and the feeling—of shared humanity. "Naturally. Come in, come in," were the words of Madame Trocmé, a French rescuer who opened her home to many Jewish refugees and, along with the villagers of the tine French town of Le Chambon-sur-Lignon, saved the lives of more than 3,000 Jews during WWII.[12] This welcome is the watchword of a worldview defined by interdependence and reciprocity, common humanity and mutual aid. On measures of social responsibility, altruistic moral reasoning, empathic concern, and risk-taking, rescuers have been found to differ from bystanders by more than three standard deviations.[13] But Monroe believes that more important than any of these characteristics is the overriding "sense of one's self in relation to other people." This idea so thoroughly shaped the character of rescuers that they "genuinely could not "see" any other option than to help their fellow human beings. To do otherwise was, literally, unimaginable."[14]

Rescue behavior then was not a matter of virtue or obligation; it was a matter of a relational worldview and the perception of self in relation to others that follows from it. One author recalls telling a group of rescuers from Le Chambon that he thought they were "good people." Their response was to laugh in amazement. "They saw no alternative to their actions and to the way they acted, and therefore they saw what they did as necessary, not something to be picked out for praise. Helping these guests was for them as natural as breathing or eating-one does not think of alternatives to these functions."[15] So profoundly shaped were they by their sense of connection with other human beings that rescue activity was simply an expression of who they were. It is for this reason that rescuers tend to describe their actions as "ordinary," as what a decent person ought to do—and can do.

This self-assessment is true of rescuers who acted during times of genocide and those who act under less extreme historical circumstances. Monroe tells the story of a San Diego man who literally saved a child from the jaws of a mountain lion. "He tracked the mountain lion down, picked up a big stick and started attacking it so the mountain lion would get mad at him and drop the child." But when asked to talk about his deed, the man emphatically disputed his heroism: "'No! I didn't want this award. I didn't do anything unusual and I shouldn't have gotten an award. It's what everyone should do.'"[16]

Teaching Rescue Literature in the Context of Sustainability

Though we don't know for sure how any of us will react in extreme circumstances—a point the psychiatrist Bruno Bettleheim made in his reflections on the Nazi concentration camps—we do know that our decisions are not indiscriminate. They are, to a great extent, consistent with our self-understanding and the moral narrative that informs this identity. Though there are no demographic generalizations that help us to understand rescuers—not age, religious affiliation, wealth, education, politics or profession—we know that rescuers differed from bystanders in their perception of their relation to others and in their sense of agency.

It is not, then, sheer accident that some people become rescuers and others don't. The fact that rescuers and bystanders have a profoundly different sense of relationality and agency makes the study of rescue behavior relevant to the teaching of sustainability. For the word "sustainability" stretches beyond the objective study of environmental science and engineering, design and technology. It extends to ethical preserves, to the hope and desire for ecological civilizations, structured in ways that make justice and care normative and that strengthen life-supporting relations with the natural world. This is the vision at the core of sustainability studies and it is why the study of goodness is fundamental to the teaching of sustainability. To study rescue behavior within classes in sustainability is to acknowledge that the field of sustainability is grounded in an ethical commitment conjoined with the responsibility to educate students who understand what needs to be done and who feel, as rescuers did, compelled to act.

For years, philosopher Philip Hallie studied cruelty, violence, and evil. It took a toll on his psychological health. When he turned his attention to the Nazi experiments on children, he found himself alternating between hatred and despair and courting depression. He recalls the day he contemplated suicide, sunk in mental darkness, and then, the passage in a book that saved him. It was the story of the tiny village of Le Chambon-sur-Lignon in southern France where residents saved the lives of more than 3,000 Jews during WWII. Hallie redirected his work to the study of goodness, giving it the kind of attention that is too often reserved for evil, documenting the practice of goodness as vividly as Mengele's vicious experiments had been documented.

In classes on sustainability, I have assigned Hallie's book, In the Eye of the Hurricane: Tales of Good and Evil, Help and Harm and Paul Rusesabagina's harrowing autobiography, An Ordinary Man, about his successful effort to protect his family and 1,268 Hutu and Tutsi refugees during the Rwandan genocide. They are "case studies" in goodness, examples of decency under indecent conditions. Like all good literature, these works are invitations to intimacy. In giving us access to the interior decisions that shape a private life, they coax us to consider the nooks and crannies of our own ethical commitments and the measure of our own ethical strength. In the courses, we tried to understand why rescuers were willing to risk their lives to protect strangers, what they believed about themselves and others, their values, identity, sense of agency, and how they chose to act. What did rescuers do and how did they find the strength to do it? Could I do what they did? Students reported that they were not only deeply moved by these stories; they were fortified in their desire to be good.

The study of rescue behavior is not the study of heroes who are singularly able to transcend conventional behavior. If rescuers are presented in this way, we reinforce a worldview of radical individualism—and grant ourselves dispensation for inaction. And we hide the important truth that rescue efforts almost always depend on a network of relations and strong community bonds. Rescue literature instead, invites us to examine our understanding of the configuration of life and how this shapes identity and behavioral expectations. This knowledge is fundamental to our inquiry into sustainability and our efforts to chart paths for promoting the wellbeing of life. The principles of interrelatedness and intrinsic worth of all life—the unshakable first principles of rescuers— are very clearly the fundamental elements of an ecological worldview. They challenge the radical individualism, reductionism, and mechanism of the modern worldview. And they challenge the dominant social science theory that human behavior follows the rule of maximizing utility in which decisions are governed by the desire to increase personal advantage. Rescuer behavior—and indeed, all altruistic behavior—contradicts this model. Rescuers understand themselves as members of a network of relations and as part of a fellowship of human beings. This relational worldview overlaps entirely with an ecological worldview in which the aim is to live companionably in the world.

We live in a world in the throes of severe environmental decline and at risk of monumental social upheaval. These are factors that fuel genocide. As much as we teach students about alternative economic systems or sustainable agriculture or urban redesign, we must also give attention to what humans are capable of doing—both good and bad—and provide models for increasing ethical agency. Our social fabric is shaped by the stories we tell each other. To hear stories only about evil and not also about goodness hinders our ability to develop patterns of kindness and love, modes of relation on which culture depends. Stories of moral agency exercised in turbulent times can help students become the kinds of people they want to be and do the good work they want to do in a world that is fast approaching ecological chaos. As surely as we need to teach about the material aspects of the state of the world, we need to cultivate what the writer Terry Tempest Williams calls "an active heart." Rescuers give witness to the possibilities of self-determination and the fact that there is a kind of power that is different from the destructive power of perpetrators and the self-deceiving power of bystanders. Teaching patterns of behavior and thinking that enable people to be rescuers is a way to counter the narcissistic tendencies of many students, to help them develop a moral imagination that transcends self-absorption and indifference, and to prepare them to participate in the building of those structures of goodness that will support ecological civilizations.If we are to achieve these goals, we need to make the study of goodness and the emotional repertoire that includes compassion, altruism, and moral agency a part of what it means to be ecologically literate.

References

1 Wendell Berry, quoted in N.Y. Times, "Out on the Prairie, Moon, Music and Lectures, Too," Kathryn Shattuck, Oct. 2, 2012, http://www.nytimes.com/2012/10/03/us/prairie-festival-draws-crowds-to-land-institute-in-kansas.html?_r=1& (accessed April 4, 2014).

2 Ibid, p. 230

3 Ibid, p. 373, footnote 24

4 "Ecological values, narcissism, and materialism: a comparison of business students in the USA and The Netherlands," James W. Westerman, Erik Van Beek, Jennifer Westerman, Brian G. Whitaker, International Journal of Innovation and Sustainable Development, Feb. 11, 2014 (http://www.environmental-expert.com/articles/ecological-values-narcissism-and-materialism-a-comparison-of-business-students-in-the-usa-and-the-ne-413253, accessed 3/30/14).

5 Personal conversation (3/23/14) with Dr. Jim Westerman, co-author of a comparative study of Business, Sustainable Development, and Psychology students. Notably, students majoring in psychology scored below the national average on tests for narcissism.

6 "The Rising Tide of Narcissism: What B-Schools Can Do," Joe Daly and Jim Westerman, Blomberg Business Week, October 4, 2010. http://www.businessweek.com/stories/2010-10-04/the-rising-tide-of-narcissism-what-b-schools-can-dobusinessweek-business-news-stock-market-and-financial-advice (accessed March 30, 2014).

7 Wendell Berry, quoted in "A Conversation with Wendell Berry and West Jackson," by Joshua J. Yates, Hedgehog Review: Critical Reflections on Contemporary Culture, Vol 14, No. 2 (Summer, 2012). http://iasc-culture.org/THR/THR_article_2012_Summer_Interview_Berry_Jackson.php

8 Westerman, J.H., Westerman, J.W. & Whitaker, B.G. Environ Dev Sustain (2016) 18: 561. doi:10.1007/s10668-015-9665-7

9 Sara B. Algoe and Jonathan Haidt, "Witnessing excellence in action: the 'other-praising' emotions of elevation, gratitude, and admiration," Journal of Positive Psychology, 2009:4(2): 105-127. Author manuscript; available in PMC Jun 2, 2009. http://www.ncbi.nlm.nih.gov/pmc/articles/PMC2689844/?report=classic (accessed 4/6/14)

10 Monroe, op cit, 3

11 Ibid, 190-191

12 cited in Philip Hallie, In the Eye of the Hurricane: Tales of Good and Evil, Help and Harm (Middleton, CT: Wesleyan University Press, 1997), 45

13 Stephanie Fagin-Jones and Elizabeth Midlarsky (2007), "Courageous Altruism: Personal and Situational Correlates of Rescue during the Holocaust," The Journal of Positive Psychology: Dedicated to furthering research and promoting good practice, 2:2, 136-147, DOI: 10.1080/17439760701228979, p. 143.

14 Monroe, op. cit., 260

15 Philip Hallie, ""From Cruelty to Goodness," The Hastings Center Report, 1981 http://academics.triton.edu/uc/Ethics/PDF_Files/Hallie.pdf

16 See Merrily Helgeson, "Of human bonds," an interview with Kristin Monroe in Today @ UCI, http://archive.today.uci.edu/Features/profile_detail.asp?key=46 (accessed 4/13/14).

Language Matters: Cultivating Responsible Language Practices Through the EcoJustice Framework

AGNES CAROLINE KRYNSKI
EASTERN MICHIGAN UNIVERSITY

The power of language is one of the common threads running through much EcoJustice scholarship. In the field of teacher education, an EcoJustice approach allows us to help cultivate respectful and responsible language practices in prospective and practicing teachers. This is both indispensable and timely. My interest in this topic stems from two different professional endeavors in which I am engaged. I work as a foreign language teacher at a high school and as an instructor in teacher education at a university. In both instances, I take an EcoJustice approach to the content we learn. I also systematically draw my students' attention to language issues. This might seem a self-evident focus in a language acquisition class, but it is not always what students in teacher education classes expect to be learning about.

It is clear that generally no one disputes that language constitutes the central concern of language acquisition classes or language arts curricula. However when it comes to other fields, as Norman Fairclough (2015) remarks, "for most people, focusing on language will initially make little sense; the significance of language will generally need to be painstakingly demonstrated" (p. 253). It could also be argued that not thinking (or having to think) about language is a form of monolingual privilege analogous to invisible white privilege as articulated by Peggy McIntosh (1998). To heed Fairclough's admonition and to not fall into the trap of monolingual privilege, we need to acknowledge language as an essential factor in education.

The decision to address language issues in teacher education rests on several key considerations. First, that there is an ethical dimension to teaching which requires educators to challenge current frameworks of dominant language practices. Second, that speaking and writing against the dominant stream is in many ways a daunting challenge. Third, that language has generative power. Language is never static. It adapts and arises in contexts. It comes into being as a result of interactions among creatures, the elements, and our habitats (Smith, 2001; Martusewicz, 2013; Martusewicz, 2016). Language only appears solid and permanent because as it is renewed in each interaction it may change to take on the same form as before, but it changes all the same. With each new utterance there exists potential for a more just language.

Intersections between Language Teaching and Teacher Education

In this reflective essay, I write about why I have come to actively incorporate language-related topics in my teacher education courses. As a foreign language teacher, one of my primary concerns lies with the development of deliberate and thoughtful language use among my students. I want my students to respect other cultures and relate positively to different ways of speaking and being. I also want to help them uncover the perspectives that are to be found in the language systems and cultural practices in the new language and cultures they are studying. I revel in this part of teaching a language because it usually leads students to challenge what they have been taught all their lives. This approach to teaching languages is in line with scholarship in language pedagogy that calls for teaching about the ideological dimension of languages (Reagan & Osborn, 2002; Osborn, 2006). These authors argue that language study not only helps us find our common humanity, but also respect our diversity:

> Such understanding has profound implications not only epistemologically, but also with respect to developing a critical awareness of language and social relationships. In studying languages other than our own, we are seeking to understand (and, indeed, in at least a weak sense, to become) the Other-we are, in short, attempting to enter into realities that have, to some degree, been constructed by others and in which many of the fundamental assumptions about the nature of knowledge and society may be different from our own. (Reagan & Osborn, 2002, pp. 12-13)

This type of justice-informed language teaching serves as both an anchor and springboard for my own work in teacher education. As a teacher educator who takes an EcoJustice approach, I want my students to undergo a similar process so that they understand how dominant language practices benefit some more than others, mediate exclusion and reproduce social and ecological injustice. This type of language awareness, having the potential to affect behavior, is what I refer to as respectful and responsible language practices. Ultimately, I want my students in both educational settings to come to think of their language and cultural practices not as universally valid, but as the result of their participation in a particular location and at a particular moment in time.

Language, in the sense I use here, is both linguistic system and social practice. It is not set in stone, nor is it beyond critique. Thinking of language as a social practice empowers speakers and writers. It highlights that speakers get to make choices, not simply reproduce taken-for-granted language patterns. And when speakers make choices, ethical potential arises. Chet Bowers (2001) explains that "The cultural patterns shared within a language community generally are learned and reenacted at a taken-for-granted level of awareness" (p. 157). What I want my students to be able to do is to recognize harmful patterns in what is said and written and, in turn, produce language that disrupts such practices at this taken-for-granted level of awareness.

Attention to Language in EcoJustice Education

I am particularly drawn to the definition of language found in the EcoJustice framework. Language informs a cultural ecological analysis, and it is central to revitalizing the commons (Martusewicz, Edmundson, & Lupinacci, 2015). According to Martusewicz et al. (2015), language is "a complex and creative process of differentiation that makes all meaning possible" (p. 58). In this view, language as a "complex symbolic system" (Martusewicz et al., 2015, p. 58) makes particular ways of thinking about the world and our place in it more salient than others. For example, we might have students observe to what extent how we think about nature is mediated through the way we speak and write about nature. To that end, Martusewicz et al. (2015) state that, "if our language map tells us that humans are separate from nature, it becomes difficult or impossible for us to see our interdependence with the natural world" (p. 61). In essence, the EcoJustice framework examines dominant discourses and identifies root metaphors as symptoms of deeply held beliefs about the world.

EcoJustice Education offers educators the opportunity to orient their students toward responsible language practices because it attends to intersecting environmental and social concerns through a pedagogy of responsibility (Martusewicz et al., 2015). As a practicing teacher, I am reminded daily that such an all-encompassing vision of pedagogy cannot be handed to teachers in the form of ready-made curriculum materials, but that it should emerge experientially out of sustained local educational practice. It must arise out of the lived experience, including the language practices, of teachers and students. Martusewicz et al. (2015) explain that a pedagogy of responsibility needs to be "enacted" (p. 128). This process can begin formally in teacher education courses when students solidify their vision of what kinds of teachers they want to become.

EcoJustice oriented teacher educators help their students develop a deep understanding of the consequences of various language practices. Bowers and Martusewicz (2009) write that "to understand the cultural and environmental commons, students need language that more accurately represents the complex nature of traditions" (p. 274) and that "language now reproduces the thought patterns and values of the industrial culture" (Bowers & Martusewicz, 2009, p. 277). These scholars maintain that this comprises "the continuities within the culture that are examples of nonmonetized activities, relationships, and forms of knowledge that protect the land and the human communities living on it" (Bowers & Martusewicz, 2009, p. 274). Such an outlook imbues language with generative potential. We need to adopt such a dynamic view of language in order to garner this generative potential for educational purposes and processes.

Practicing Language

In common parlance, the word "practice" can refer to the application of theory or repeated activity. We practice a sport or playing an instrument. Practice often implies long duration and improvement of a skill. Alastair Pennycook's (2010) work on "language as a local practice" expands on this everyday use of the word. Pennycook (2010) and others scholars in critical applied linguistics, critical discourse studies, and ethics mirror EcoJustice scholars' interest in a dynamic view of language. Understanding language as an ever-evolving set of language practices makes intervention possible. According to Pennycook (2010), "practices prefigure activity: they are not reducible to things we do, but rather are the organizing principle behind them" (p. 29). This approach views language and identity as arising out of and constantly being renewed through relationships and material and social practices.

Speakers and writers are not passive users but active constructors of language. Pennycook (2010) continues, "language . . . becomes a social practice, as are language teaching, translation and language policy; such practices operate above the level of activity and below the level of social order, as mediators of how things are done" (p. 29). In this view, language practices inform speakers and writers. And speakers and writers sustain and modify language practices in turn. This conceptualization of language differs from a view of language as a sort of passed-down inheritance, a notion that impedes the search for alternative language practices. Such an image of language as a system of strict rules and prescriptions is an academic imposition. It might even largely stem from the way we teach grammar in language acquisition and language arts classes, more than we as language educators care to admit.

In addition, reason and emotion are intricately connected at the level of language practices. We communicate our thoughts and states of mind primarily through different forms of language. Writing about dominant discourses and our personal identification with them, Underhill (2011) notes that it is "individuals, who choose to endorse it and conform to its dictates" (p. 238) and "only by their identifying with the dominant discourse can that discourse survive. Cultural mindsets, ideological worldviews, are maintained by people, and by people alone" (Underhill, 2011, p. 238). Underhill's point highlights and privileges humans as maintainers of discourses whereas Smith (2001) says that a "process of self-formation . . . is never entirely within our control since values are neither recognized nor apportioned solely through our human labor. Nature too is active in framing and constituting what becomes significant" (p. 219). In terms of language practices, both our human agency as speakers, but also our human acknowledgement of more-than-human influences on our language practices is essential. When we understand language as a set of local language practices, we are able to trace language activity to its sources.

Challenging Dominant Language Practices

As a practicing foreign language teacher, I am captivated by current events related to language policy. A current educational development relative to language in France is a fascinating example of how language issues relate to education. This is an example of how difficult it is to change language practices and language activity. At the same time, it demonstrates that there is a strong desire to attend to the harmful elements human languages carry. The issue is an attempted reform at changing French grammar to make it more gender-neutral. In French, this would involve changing the French expression "les droits de l'Homme" (the rights of man) to "les droits humains" (human rights). In addition to this more egalitarian way of conceptualizing rights, although thinkers like Rosi Braidotti also problematize a rights-based discourse that is premised on membership in humanity (Braidotti, 2013, p. 1), this reform would also eliminate other instances of the masculine generic. Proponents of this initiative call the elements of the reform "l'écriture inclusive" (inclusive writing) and "la grammaire égalitaire" (egalitarian grammar). Opponents, mainly consisting of the Académie française and other public figures, call the effort dangerous (Bouanchaud, 2017).

Speaking and writing against dominant streams is in many ways a formidable task. This is evident in the French example. Powerful institutions and influential public figures use their linguistic capital to preserve or introduce dominant, often harmful, language patterns. Because sustained immersion in such a linguistic climate, if left unchecked, reproduces values that fuel prejudice, hatred, and destruction, educators must attend to the ways in which dominant ways of speaking and writing benefit some more than others. Bowers and Martusewicz (2009) draw our attention to the fact that "the combination of silences and linguistic-based misrepresentations can distort the ability to recognize the realities of daily life" (p. 275). Children deserve teachers who take a step back before repeating commonly reproduced language patterns. At the same time, more just discursive practices require time to take root. George Lakoff (2008) explains that "change does not come overnight. Say things not once, but over and over. Brains change when ideas are repeatedly activated" (p. 116). Teachers can help their students develop more just habits of mind as a result of sustained curriculum that is infused with alternative discourses.

Educators should be aware of dominant ideologies and how they are reproduced. According to Smith (2001) in critical social theory, "every utterance takes on social import in terms of either furthering the cause of the dominant ideology or striving to fracture its uniformity" (p. 80). It might help to think of language as a symptom, but not the disease. By understanding language to hold generative power, we do not discount the importance of changing other practices and behaviors. But as educators, we should be interested in the question of how the current state of our language can become an indicator of a society that permeates with respect, kindness and affection and how language can mediate inclusion.

Teaching as a form of ethical practice requires educators to address the current makeup of dominant language practices, including the assumptions and consequences inherent in habitual ways of speaking and writing. This is what French educators are doing when they refuse to value-hierarchize gender, even in something believed to be as solid as grammar. Rosi Braidotti (2013) states that, "we need to devise new social, ethical and discursive schemes of subject formation to match the profound transformations we are undergoing. That means that we need to learn to think differently about ourselves" (p. 12). Educators can play a vital role in responding to such a call for innovative thinking, speaking, and writing.

Paying attention to language necessitates a fundamental shift in how educators conceive of their work. This shift must be based on hope for a better way of thinking, writing, and speaking about our embeddedness within the natural world. One of the ways in which educators at all levels can accomplish this is through attention to and cultivation of responsible language practices. Braidotti (2013) writes, "The pursuit of collective projects aimed at the affirmation of hope, rooted in the ordinary micro-practices of everyday life, is a strategy to set up, sustain and map out sustainable transformations" (p. 192). Educators must understand that language as such a "micro-practice" reproduces injustices of all forms on a daily basis if we do not counteract such practices.

Language Practices Worthy of our Ideals

Why is critical language awareness crucial to the educational endeavor? After all, teaching prospective teachers about curriculum, pedagogy, and social contexts can be done without asking students to contemplate the role language plays in our communities. However, it does not suffice to address only how we think and behave with the expectation that language practices will simply fall into place. If we do only that, there is the danger of teachers who may know better but unwittingly keep reproducing language patterns that reinforce values they don't even believe in anymore. But, as Underhill (2011) remarks, "the writer and literary scholar remind us that all fiercely free-thinking individuals are capable of expanding the sphere of their own intellectual freedom by pushing back the limits of their own language system at any given moment in history" (p. 6). Indeed, in an EcoJustice context, that push back might be cast as more of a collaborative endeavor, rather than just an individual pursuit, to be more effective, but Underhill's general sentiment holds true nonetheless. As a thinker, I can push back the limits of a language system that casts me as hyper isolated.

Individuals who are cognizant of their embeddedness within the natural world work together to build language practices worthy of the ideals they hold. Such thinkers keep in mind that living by just principles does not automatically equate with sustained responsible language use. As a result of being in our classes, students may come to see things differently without adjusting how they speak and write as they venture forth on their various paths. This should worry us. Both intended and unintended language use can stand in the way of just relationships. In fact, we all need to be aware of a possible disconnect between our ideals and our language practices.

The Limits of Language

It is also true that an adjustment to how we use language does not automatically lead to adjustments in our thinking and behavior. Changing language activity alone is never sufficient. As an educator, I am always concerned about the authenticity of my students' learning. When I teach, I do so in the belief that language influences our thinking, beliefs, and behavior and that discourses shape our worldviews. I am hopeful that evidence of more thoughtfulness in my students' speaking and writing about educational issues is an indication of their deep inquiry into and critical processing of the linguistic universe around them. When students show an interest in examining language practices as they materialize in our local places, I understand this to constitute a first step toward the enactment of more wide-reaching changes.

Language, of course, is not the sole carrier of potential ethical messages, even if it is often evidence of our underlying values. To a degree, language limits our field of vision. But if language completely limited our worldview, we would never be able to reach beyond the values embedded in our linguistic system. Indeed, making an effort to turn our heads to see beyond our line of vision is necessary. Undoubtedly, language is central to how we learn and teach. Undoubtedly, extra-linguistic experiences also contribute to learning and teaching. Smith (2001) calls for an ethics of place rooted in the material: "Every ethics is a *shaping* and *enframing* of the social and natural environment, it sculpts and composes a different world within the material constraints and possibilities afforded by its own particular time and place" (p. 25). And it would seem also of its language since Smith (2001) remarks,

> Language inevitably orders the world, applying systems of classification to it that both constrain and facilitate our coming to recognize parts of our environment as significant others. Theory articulates these taxonomies but the word cannot replace the world. All language only gets meaning through its participation in a "form of life" and it is this form of life and the individual's relation to it that "dictates" what *feels* right and wrong.
> (Smith, 2001, p. 208)

At the same time, Smith (2001) is generally critical of focusing strictly on language and culture as the locus of ethical decision-making. He argues that, "ethics becomes a wholly cultural phenomenon and one that can only be acknowledged insofar as it can be voiced. But nature communicates to us, and through us, in many different ways; through the early morning's light, the night's warm breeze, the bark's rough texture, the dawn chorus . . . (Smith, 2001, p. 70). This is a beautiful and vital observation about the importance of extralinguistic influences on our thinking and the communicative power of the natural world. I would argue that the way Smith communicates these experiences to us is an example of the generative power of language. Experiences that could potentially remain ephemeral become more concrete and sharable when we speak and write about them. We recognize them as worthy of being repeated. Yet, to me as a language teacher, Smith's concern about the limits of language is important.

With any solidification of experience in language, the experience itself risks being reduced to one interpretation. Understanding language in terms of local language practices (Pennycook, 2010), some of which may be non-verbal, and that allow for a multitude of interpretations can help us deal with such representational limitations.

Using words differently and reaching beyond the usual ways our culture teaches us to express ourselves, allows us to recognize to what extent natural processes have an impact on us. We may have those experiences, and they may be even more impactful than cultural experiences can be, but to share (that is, to teach) them we still use language. In fact, the same experiences of perceiving natural phenomena could be clothed in very different language and lead to very different ethical insights. On this topic, Braidotti (2013) remarks, "the collapse of the nature-culture divide requires that we need to devise a new vocabulary" (p. 82). Rebecca Martusewicz (2016) writes about education as requiring "a recognition of difference that interrupts the normalization of anthropocentric and other hierarchized ways of relating to one another and the more-than-human world" (p. 72). We can clearly see these ways of relating externalized in how we speak and write, and we can ask our students to question the authority of any harmful dominant language practices. This is not an easy process. Braidotti (2013) explains, "the challenge for critical theory is momentous: we need to visualize the subject as a transversal entity encompassing the human, our genetic neighbors the animals and the earth as a whole, and to do so within an understandable language" (p. 82). I would maintain that with our focus on making the complex more accessible to learners, working on such a language should also be part of the responsibilities of educators.

Rethinking language practices and language activity on ethical grounds is in essence a decentering practice similar to learning a second language.

As Michael McCarthy (2015) writes,

> . . . at the heart of our notions of good and bad lies human suffering, and what we can do to avoid it. This is so deep-rooted in us now, so instinctive, that it has been internalised in the language: one of our most prized virtues is humanity, one of our deepest tributes to another person, that they are humane… Our morality now is entirely anthropocentric: we automatically define objective good by what is best for ourselves. So where humanity's interests clash with other interests, the other are likely to get short shrift from us, even when they involve proper functioning of the planet, which is the only place we have to live. (McCarthy, 2015, p. 20)

McCarthy draws our attention to the internalization of beliefs in language. Here, too, self-serving language can be understood to be a symptom of human hubris. With this observation, another paradox emerges: the internalization of beliefs is at once an externalization because language does not hide its harmful elements that well. What is internalized is simultaneously externalized. All it takes is often to brush away the settled dust that lightly obscures harmful language practices. Once we help our students see language differently, to expose the buried ideologies behind dominant ways of expressing ourselves, they can learn to generate more just language practices. We can overcome some of the limits language places on our ability to perceive ourselves as part of nature.

The Generative Power of Language

Thus, in our efforts to critique dominant language practices, we cannot forget that language has generative power. Educators must teach about how to resist undemocratic ideologies by actively choosing to use language that promotes kindness and respect. The French example of inclusive writing efforts is a good example of how changing language habits can potentially bring about changes in perceptions and behavior. Pennycook (2010) explains that "once we accept that language is a social practice, it becomes clear that it is not language form that governs the speakers of the language but rather the speakers that negotiate what possible language forms they want to use for what purpose" (p. 129). This fruitful definition of what language accomplishes helps us formulate a vision of speakers and writers who transcend dominant ways of speaking and writing that are so clearly symptomatic of deeper underlying problems with our very values.

This is in line with EcoJustice Education's focus on challenging unhealthy ways of thinking. Martusewicz et al. (2015) state, "Language shapes thought, but it is always possible to shift how we think and thus how we behave re relative to one another by using different ways of describing or representing the world" (Martusewicz et al., 2015, p. 68). The EcoJustice framework with its focus on uncovering the damaging legacies of Western rationalist discourses can provide a counter-discourse strategy for primary and secondary schools, universities and other educational learning communities. As an approach that seeks to uncover assumptions, EcoJustice Education is also in line with the concept of sustainability literacy. Stibbe and Luna (2009) remark that,

> As people gain sustainability literacy skills, they become empowered to read society critically, discovering insights into the unsustainable trajectory that the society is on and the social structures that underpin this trajectory. But more than this, they become empowered to engage with those social structures and contribute to the re-writing of self and society along more sustainable lines. (Stibbe & Luna, 2009, p. 11)

This "critical reading" of society is essentially about being aware of the many functions of language and the way languages can be employed for different purposes. The generative aspect of social critique is also put front and center when Stibbe and Luna refer here to a "re-writing of self and society" (Stibbe & Luna, 2009, p. 11).

Tensions between Different Language Practices

I maintain throughout this essay that language, in its complexity, deserves the attention of teacher educators and prospective and practicing teachers. How they can accomplish an integration of language awareness into teacher education more effectively by placing language issues center stage merits closer examination. But should the creation of new discourses be our only aim? On the one hand, as Braidotti (2013) points out, old thinking and language patterns no longer suffice to address current and future challenges. On the other hand, Wendell Berry (1983) admonishes us about the loss of valuable language patterns.

> My impression is that we have seen, for perhaps a hundred and fifty years, a gradual increase in language that is either meaningless or destructive of meaning. And I believe that this increasing unreliability of language parallels the increasing disintegration, over the same period, of persons and communities. (Berry, 1983, p. 24)

In a similar vein, Pennycook (2018) writes that "this rediscovery of the commons, of the need for collective action, concern about the environment, reorientation to the more-than-human world-all this has been a concern, a knowledge, of Indigenous people around the world for a long time" (p. 143). Educators need to work toward reinstating such respectful and responsible language practices.

This work can begin as soon as we ask ourselves some vital questions. How will I as an educator address outdated language patterns and generate new ones with my students? Likewise, to what extent will we work to recover meaningful language patterns now on the brink of extinction? Teacher educators who care about ecological and social justice must engage practicing and prospective teachers around such difficult questions.

Paying attention to language also involves paying attention to students' language use. Writing about the importance of understanding and respecting dialect differences in students, Joanne Dowdy (2002) states that

> The war will be won when she who is marginalized comes to speak more in her own language, and people accept her communication as valid and representative. Her need to communicate, formerly unhappy forays into the unfamiliar territory of alternate language discourse, will blossom into the flowers that had been dormant in the arid land of the desert of master discourse. (Dowdy, 2002, p. 13)

Here, Dowdy makes clear that not only does language influence our values, but that our perception of students' learning is influenced by prejudice about their language use, i.e. how they express themselves is seen as inferior. Osborn's (2006) insistence on language reproducing power relations in society or Dowdy's (2002) observations about classroom discourse shaping students' identities as inferior or superior in relation to others are all parts of the educational puzzle of which prospective and practicing teachers must be made aware. Furthermore, Betsy Rymes (2016) explains that classroom discourse can lead to the "systematic exclusion of certain students" (p.2). We need to both look at language at the macro as well as the micro levels of interaction. Paying attention to language helps us uncover these particular linguistic injustices and better understand all forms of injustice as we consider present educational realities.

Language Awareness in Teacher Education

Traditionally, learning to teach is conceived of as fundamentally being about the learning of skills. Teaching skills include classroom management skills, lesson planning skills, and communication skills, but also more all-encompassing analytic and literacy skills. But, teacher education should be more than that. We must teach in support of just relationships and in respect of our embeddedness in the natural world. To accomplish this, EcoJustice Education does not shy away from bringing intellectually challenging theory to prospective teachers' attention.

An ecological cultural analysis is based on understanding centric thinking. This type of thinking is "the tendency to give higher value to a concept that is more "central" than another, as in the example, androcentrism (male-centeredness), which puts man as more central or important/valuable than woman" (Martusewicz et al., 2015, p. 92). Centric thinking manifests itself in centric language practices. Braidotti (2013) remarks that,

> ...by organizing differences on a hierarchical scale of decreasing worth, this humanist subject defined himself as much by what he excluded from, as by what he included in, his self-representation, an approach which often justified a violent and belligerent relationship to the sexualized, racialized and naturalized 'others' that occupied the slot of devalued difference. (Braidotti, 2013, p. 144)

Teachers need to be aware of how centric thinking underlies dominant language practices. Taking this into consideration might be helpful for French educators as they attempt to implement gender-neutral language.

Once we are clear on why we need to focus on language in teacher education, a foray into applied linguistics might yield some fruitful finds. The EcoJustice framework encourages critical discourse studies as a qualitative method of inquiry. The field of critical discourse studies combines language awareness, social theory, and ethics. At this generative nexus, teacher educators can find ways in which to address language issues in their classes. According to Wodak and Meyer (2016) critical discourse studies "approaches are characterized by the common interests in deconstructing ideologies and power through the systematic . . . investigation of semiotic data (written, spoken or visual)" (p. 4). As with sustainability literacy as articulated by Stibbe and Luna (2009), critical discourse studies can be a method that helps educators understand the consequences of the choices we make in speaking and writing and help us generate better ways of relating to others.

Many scholars take language issues seriously and include them as part of their content analysis. Teacher educators must encourage prospective teachers to familiarize themselves with scholarship that acknowledges the power of language. For example, social studies teachers might want to read Scott Kurashige's work. Kurashige (2017) writes about racial conflict in the United States and simultaneously focuses the reader's attention on how language is used to influence thinking and how certain events (here, the Detroit Rebellion of 1967) are framed using deliberately chosen language that evokes fear (here, riots): "counter-revolutionary forces, however, upended the political will for progressive or radical social change. Insisting that the urban disturbances be called 'riots'"(Kurashige, 2017, p. 8). Furthermore, Kurashige (2017) remarks that, "the suburban 'family values' discourse was further sustained by projecting transgressive behavior onto Detroit" (p. 39). Kurashige's work abounds with examples of critical language awareness (Fairclough, 2015). This type of linguistic content analysis (reminiscent of critical discourse studies) illuminates issues that would otherwise not stand out to the learner.

In a similar manner, educators in the biological and environmental sciences can make connections to language extinction. In scholarship that demonstrates how the loss of ecological and linguistic diversity is linked, Daniel Nettle and Suzanne Romaine (2000) write about, "many striking similarities between the loss of linguistic diversity and the loss of biodiversity" (p. 16). They remark that, "extinctions in general, whether of languages or species, are part of a more general pattern of human activities contributing to radical alterations in our ecosystems" (Nettle & Romaine, 2000, p. 16). If teacher educators expose prospective and practicing teachers to such analyses, these teachers will learn to think critically about language and communicate their insights to their own students.

Language Awareness and the Construction of Teaching Philosophies

Teacher education from an EcoJustice framework is invested in the construction of ethically-informed teaching philosophies. Constructing a teaching philosophy for oneself can be thought of as telling a story about teaching. Stibbe (2015) explains,

> The purpose of revealing, exposing or shedding light on the stories-we-live-by is to open them up to question and challenge- are these stories working in the current conditions of the world or do we need to search for new stories? Whether or not the stories are considered to be 'working' depends on the ethical vision of the analyst, i.e. on whether the stories are building the kind of world that the analyst wants to see. (Stibbe, 2015, pp. 10-11)

Thus, a teaching philosophy needs to be based on complex ethical considerations. As teachers construct their teaching philosophies, they need to think about to what extent dominant language practices inform their own understanding of teaching and learning and how they speak and write about educational practice. Writing about the purposes of education, Martusewicz et al. (2015) argue that,

> ...the purpose of public education must be to develop citizens who can actively work toward a democratic and sustainable society, one that values cultural diversity for what it offers to community problem solving and for the essential role that biodiversity plays in the very possibility of living systems (Martusewicz et al., 2015, p. 22).

The EcoJustice framework and courses aligned with it, insist that students articulate a vision of what education ought to be like in a diverse, democratic, and sustainable society (Martusewicz et al, 2015). As teaching philosophies often include ruminations on how the writer conceives of teaching as a profession, teachers must contemplate the nature and purpose of their work and the language practices that are part of any teaching practice. When teacher educators ask their students to consider the consequences of various language practices, they teach students the importance of attending to language issues as part of their own educational practice.

Language Practices Matter

When contemplating the transition from teaching a foreign language to teaching courses in teacher education, I can't help but understand one activity in terms of the other. I have found that paying attention to language is valuable in both roles. As a long-time language educator, I will not ever be able to truly disengage from thinking of teaching as the teaching of an alternative way of speaking and writing and, thus, another way of understanding the world. In fact, as I maintain in this essay, teacher education courses focused on schools in a diverse, democratic and sustainable society should engage students in thinking about language. We must encourage resistance to negative discourses and, at the same time, foster the development of positive discourses. Our students need to be aware of the different language practices that follow from these discourses.

Attention to language as a set of local language practices can lead to new ways of speaking and thinking. This approach can fulfill Braidotti's call for innovative subject formations (Braidotti, 2013) and Smith's appeal for an "ethics of place" (Smith, 2001). Attention to language as it has changed (Berry, 1983; Pennycook, 2018) can lead to reclaiming what has been lost. With this tension between creating new discourses (Braidotti, 2013) and reclaiming discourses that have been lost (Berry, 1983; Bowers & Martusewicz, 2009; Pennycook, 2018) in mind, we must ask learners to consider what language choices we need to make on a daily basis when we teach for ecological and social justice. We need to call on teachers to become responsible language practitioners.

In line with Smith's (2001) critique of a mere culture-based ethics, what is there to do when words fail us? What methods are best suited to address research questions that involve thinking about language and education? Thinking about the intertwining of language and culture should become a central concern of educators. Due to the centrality of language in education and in social life, scholarship coming out of discourse studies (Fairclough, 2003; Gee, 2014; Rogers, 2011; Wodak & Meyer, 2016) can be helpful to teacher educators who are interested in furthering their understanding of the power of language in education. In a similar manner, scholarship in ethics (Braidotti, 2013; Smith, 2001) can also help teacher educators elucidate language issues as those relate to social and environmental contexts.

To accomplish this, we need more theory in teacher education, not less. In a neoliberal context in which time is money, asking prospective students to write pages upon pages of their vision for education is an increasingly more difficult idea to "sell." Yet, as a practicing teacher myself, I know that having a strong vision is what sustains me in my work. We need to ask why before we delve into the how of teaching. We need to understand that language is renewed through language practices, and that there are discourses and organizing principles behind language activity (Pennycook, 2010; Pennycook, 2018). We need to pay more attention to language practices, not less. This is what I tell my students who may doubt that a more theoretical look at discourses and language practices is useful to their future lives as teachers.

Braidotti (2013) maintains, "hope is a way of dreaming up possible futures: an anticipatory virtue that permeates our lives and activates them. It is a powerful motivating force…" (p. 192). Hope as an anticipatory virtue in Braidotti's sense sends a strong message to educators about the need to articulate, to speak and write for a better now and a better future. When educating for healthy and just communities, we teach away from prejudice and toward fairness, away from disrespect and toward reverence, away from egoism and toward care, and away from self-centered individualism and toward altruistic individuality.

In order to break down hierarchies and increase awareness of the multitude of needs that must be met in our communities, we need ways of thinking and decision-making that will help us to commit to a standard of well-being for all. In order to articulate these responsible ways of thinking and decision-making, educators need to model and cultivate responsible language practices. Language carries consequential meanings and how we express ourselves is very telling about what values we hold. Leaving no expression or metaphor unturned and unchallenged should be a priority for educators no matter their subject area. Ethically-grounded language shapes our thinking, connects to larger discourses and can contribute to more just habits of mind.

References

Berry, W. (1983). *Standing by words*. Berkeley, CA: Counterpoint.

Bouanchaud, C. (2017, November 24). Cinq idées reçues sur l'écriture inclusive. *Le Monde*. Retrieved from http//www.lemonde.fr

Bowers, C.A. (2001). *Educating for eco-justice and community*. Athens, GA: University of Georgia Press.

Bowers, C.A. (2006). *Revitalizing the commons: Cultural and educational sites of resistance and affirmation*. Lanham, MD: Lexington Books.

Bowers, C.A., & Martusewicz, R. A. (2009). Ecojustice and social justice. In E.F. Provenzo & A. Baker Provenzo (Eds.), *Encyclopedia of the Social and Cultural Foundations of Education*. (pp. 273-279). Thousand Oaks, CA: SAGE Publications.

Braidotti, R. (2013). *The Posthuman*. Cambridge: Polity Press.

Dowdy, J. K. (2002). Ovuh Dyuh. In L. Delpit & J. K. Dowdy (Eds.), *The skin that we speak: Thoughts on language and culture in the classroom* (p. 3-13). New York, NY: The New Press.

Fairclough, N. (2003). *Analyzing discourse: Textual analysis for social research*. London: Routledge.

Fairclough, N. (2010). *Critical Discourse Analysis: The critical study of language*. London: Routledge.

Fairclough, N. (2015). *Language and power* (3rd ed.). New York, NY: Routledge.

Gee, P. (2014). *An introduction to discourse analysis: Theory and method* (4th ed.). London: Routledge.

Kurashige, S. (2017). *The fifty-year rebellion: How the U.S. political crisis began in Detroit*. Oakland, CA: University of California Press.

Lakoff, G. (2008). *The political mind: A cognitive scientist's guide to your brain and its politics*. New York, NY: Penguin Books.

Martusewicz, R. A. (2006). Eros in the commons: Educating for eco-ethical consciousness in a poetics of place. *Ethics, Place & Environment: A Journal of Philosophy & Geography, 8*(3), 331-348.

Martusewicz, R A., Edmundson, J., & Lupinacci, J. (2015). *EcoJustice education: Toward diverse, democratic, and sustainable communities* (2nd ed.). New York, NY: Routledge.

Martusewicz, R.A. (2016). Education for eco-ethical becoming: Reading Bateson and Deleuze on difference. In W. M. Reynolds & J.A. Webber (Eds.), *Expanding curriculum theory: Dis/positions and lines of flight* (pp.62-76). New York, NY: Routledge.

McCarthy, M. (2015). *The moth snowstorm: Nature and joy*. London: John Murray Publishers.

McIntosh, P. (1998). White privilege: Unpacking the invisible knapsack. In P.S. Rothenberg (Ed.), *Race, class, and gender in the United States: An integrated study*. New York, NY: St Martin's Press.

Nettle, D., & Romaine, S. (2000). *Vanishing voices: The extinction of the world's languages*. New York, NY: Oxford University Press.

Osborn, T. A. (2006). *Teaching world languages for social justice: A sourcebook of principles and practices*. Mahwah, NJ: Lawrence Erlbaum Associates.

Pennycook, A. (2010). *Language as a local practice*. London: Routledge.

Pennycook, A. (2018). *Posthumanist applied linguistics*. London: Routledge.

Reagan, T. G. & Osborn, T. A. (2002). *The foreign language educator in society: Toward a critical pedagogy*. New York, NY: Lawrence Erlbaum Associates.

Rogers, R. (Ed.). (2011). *An introduction to Critical Discourse Analysis in education*, (2nd ed.). New York, NY: Routledge.

Rymes, B. (2016). *Classroom discourse analysis: A tool for critical reflection*. New York, NY: Routledge.

Plumwood, V. (2002). *Environmental culture*. London: Routledge.

Smith, M. (2001). *An ethics of place: Radical ecology, postmodernity and social theory*. Albany, NY: State University of New York Press.

Stibbe, A., & Luna, H. (2009). Introduction. In A. Stibbe (Ed.), *The handbook of sustainability literacy: Skills for a changing world* (pp. 9-16). Cambridge: Green Books.

Stibbe, A. (2015). *Ecolinguistics: Language, ecology and the stories we live by*. London: Routledge.

Underhill, J. W. (2011). *Creating worldviews: Metaphor, ideology and language*. Edinburgh: Edinburgh University Press.

Wodak, R., & Myer, M. (Eds.). (2016). *Methods of critical discourse studies* (3rd ed.). London: Sage Publications.

www.ingramcontent.com/pod-product-compliance
Lightning Source LLC
Chambersburg PA
CBHW081203020426
42333CB00020B/2609